# Shattered, Broken
# Restored by Grace

# SHATTERED, BROKEN RESTORED BY GRACE

### Mary's Story of the Amazing Power of Forgiveness

## Tracy Liller

ELM HILL

A Division of
HarperCollins Christian Publishing

www.elmhillbooks.com

### Shattered, Broken Restored by Grace
#### Mary's Story of the Amazing Power of Forgiveness

Published in Nashville, Tennessee, by Elm Hill, an imprint of Thomas Nelson. Elm Hill and Thomas Nelson are registered trademarks of HarperCollins Christian Publishing, Inc.

Elm Hill titles may be purchased in bulk for educational, business, fund-raising, or sales promotional use. For information, please e-mail SpecialMarkets@ ThomasNelson.com.

#### Library of Congress Cataloging-in-Publication Data

Library of Congress Control Number: 2018966482

ISBN 978-1-400324972 (Paperback)
ISBN 978-1-400324989 (eBook)

# CONTENTS

# CHAPTER 1

# WHERE DID THAT VAN COME FROM?

This day started as many others had before. I am a grandmother of eight beautiful little angels. I have four from my son, Delbert, named after his father. Their ages range from infant to five years old. My daughter, Shelby has two, both toddlers and my other daughter Lai Oshae has two, a one year old and a three year old. It's been my practice to make myself available to help out whenever they need me and lighten the load and take the kids when they need a break or have other commitments. This was one of those days. Lai Oshae lives over four hours away, so we had agreed to meet half way so I could get her girls for a few days. Lai Oshae had committed to work overtime and her weekend babysitter was having surgery. My husband and I do not get many opportunities to have these two grandkids, so we were looking forward to the next few days.

The drive was going very well and about two hours into it, I was getting close to our meeting point. Lai Oshae had picked a rendezvous spot where we could meet and split each of our drive in half. I had not driven this route before, so was not familiar with the road or the exit that I was to take. There were several things I had done on this ride that were unusual for me, but I now believe were directed by God's hand of grace. One was

1

I had put my phone in my purse. This was not a habit of mine, but I expected Lai Oshae to text me when she arrived at our meeting point to see where I was. I did not want the distraction or the temptation to look at my phone. Next, I had set my cruise control to the speed limit. A few weeks prior I had been pulled over when I was bringing another set of grandkids home. My five year old, Marina had me captivated in one of her delightful stories and I hadn't noticed a speed reduction on the road. The police officer had been very kind and understanding and I had assured him I would be extra careful in the future. I took this commitment to him seriously and started setting my cruise and paying more careful attention. Again, I believe this all to be part of God's design. The third highly unusual thing was I had my radio turned off. I had taken advantage of the peaceful ride to talk to God about some things in my life that had been weighing heavy on my heart. This may seem insignificant to many, but I had known several people who had accidents because they were messing with the radio. Now, let me help you understand why these little things stand out to me. The events that were about to follow are a blur to me. There is much of it that is a total blank. I was about to be involved in the most serious, life altering event of my life. A car wreck that I would be responsible for. I would have no memory or realization of why or how this would occur. In the aftermath, this unknowing would haunt me, but these few facts would give me a small sense that God could have possibly been looking out for me, that maybe, just maybe there was a chance that I hadn't been "grossly negligent" in the actions leading to the horrific event that was to follow.

I was going approximately 60 miles an hour, in an express lane on an interstate. I had crossed over to the express lanes, but as soon as I had I regretted the decision. Realizing not all exits are going to come off of the express lane, I had decided to get off the next chance I got. I had glanced over to the other lanes. That traffic was a little heavier than where I was but did not seem bad. I know my attention was on the road as I waited for a chance to move over. That's the last thing I remember, the last thing until... BOOM!! It sounded like an explosion, felt like one too! My vision was totally encompassed by what I thought was a brick wall. A mass of dark red filled my windshield. What is a wall doing in the middle of an expressway?! What just happened? Why am I stopped? Why does my head hurt? It's so strange when shock sets in how your brain tries to sort reality from fiction. How you try to make sense of senselessness. It seems that minutes are going by, but in reality it's mere seconds. Seconds where time stands still but the world out there is rushing in a panic!

Then, real life starts to merge with my perception. There is a man, frantic, banging on my window. "Are you okay? Get out, you need to get out! Now!"

As I look over to him I realize cars are buzzing by me. My truck is still sitting in the right lane and traffic in the left lane is traveling very quickly, 65-70 miles an hour beside me! I am sitting in what could be a death trap! I scoot over to the passenger door and slide out. This is the last time I will see my truck. The last time I care about my truck, from this moment Mary, the driver of "the other car", will be where 100% of my attention is focused.

I was in the express lane, which meant there was a grass median to my right. As I slid out my door I saw it. I saw her! I hit a van! I had been involved in a couple serious car accidents in my life, but never had another car been involved. It hadn't occurred to me that another person could have been affected here.

There were four other people running around the burgundy (brick red) van, two men, two women- all trying to get in to help her. I ran to the van with them, equally as urgent to get to her. I could see her through her window. She was obviously not conscience, laid back in her seat, mouth open, eyes closed. It did not look good. We need to get to her right now! She needs us! She needs help! What happened?! How did this happen? It doesn't matter right now- get in there and help her! Please God, Please God!! Help her!! What happened, Oh God, What did I do?!! Please God…

We ran around to the back of the van, the window had been busted out by the collision, so one of the men made it through the crumpled metal and broken glass to the inside of the vehicle. He made his way to a door lock and unlocked the doors, I almost followed him through the mangled wreck, but it seemed way too difficult and realizing the doors had been unlocked I rushed to the driver's door and got to Mary. (I later came to know her name, but even at this moment she was not just a random victim, but a real person, someone I felt a real connection to. She was a part of me now, my sister, my best friend- I don't know how to explain it, but at this moment and for many to come Mary was all that mattered to me in my life.)

The gentleman who had climbed through the back was very calm, in control, amazing in a crisis. I wondered if he was an off duty EMT or police officer. He quickly started CPR, and I so wanted to help. I had taken CPR several times, as a fitness instructor and again as a foster parent. I knew what to do. I started to place my hands on her chest to start compressions and had no strength in my right hand. It had taken blunt force in the impact and would not function. It didn't seem to matter, he was very competent and had CPR well at hand. He had shouted for us to try to find pulse. As I heard "No pulse here, do you have it?" "Not here either, no pulse, no pulse!" My heart raced, fear was taking over. I lay on Mary, holding her. "Please God don't take her, please not like this!" "Please! Please! If she doesn't know you don't let her die! What did I do? What did I do? I killed her!! I killed her!! Please God, Oh God Please! No!" I was praying, pleading, praying- holding her not wanting to let go! I felt one of the ladies there pulling me back. Stop, I'm not letting go of her, she needs me... I need her! She pulled harder, pulling me away and hugging me, holding me as I screamed and sobbed "I killed her!"

She had a calming voice "No, no it's okay. It was just an accident."

"Did you see it?! Do you know what happened? How did this happen? Where did she come from? How did she get there? Please tell me how this could happen!"

Her calm voice again resonated through my trauma "Maybe she had a heart attack, maybe her van was stopped because she passed out."

Oh, maybe, just maybe her van was there randomly. Maybe she had a health issue causing her to stop suddenly in the middle of the interstate. Is it possible? Is it possible this isn't my fault? Maybe, just maybe it's a true freak accident. I started to calm a little. My hysteria was turning to mere despair. The panic was waning just a little. But I still need to be with her, "Please let me go be with her!"

"No, they need to work on her, let them help her." I could see them, just a few feet from me. I could still hear them checking for pulse, counting as they did compressions. "No pulse, no pulse." I had settled enough to know she was right. The ambulances and police had started to arrive.

Later I realized this witness knew what had happened, Mary did not randomly stop in the road ahead of me. She was part of a long line of stopped traffic, backed up waiting to exit, a long line of cars that somehow I completely missed. I didn't see brake lights. I didn't even slow down. I will never know why.

The EMTs arrived and went to Mary. One of them stopped to see me. There were police cars nearby. I heard someone shout to close off the highway. Someone had gotten my purse and phone... or had I? I didn't remember getting them, but I had it in my hand and I heard a voice "Is there someone you can call?" Someone I can call? Oh. I was meeting Lai Oshae, she must wonder where I am. How long has it been? It feels like a lifetime, but it couldn't have been long. "Um, yeah. I need to call my husband" ... but the lady, I don't want to be away from her! I again became focused on her. She needed me with her. I wanted to be with her. But as I looked around at her, the police cars, people all rushing around her van, the reality hit me again. I killed her! I hit the speed dial button to call my husband. I heard his voice but I was in a fog. I can't really remember what he said or what I said. He later told me that all he heard was screaming "I killed her! I killed her!"

The police officer approached me "Are you the driver of the truck involved?"

"Yes, I am. Do you know what happened? Did anyone see it? Can they tell me what happened?" I was hopeful, anxious to have answers, any answers.

My air bag had not deployed. My head hit something, most likely the steering wheel and was swelling rapidly. My eye was starting to narrow to a slit and bruising was setting in. I was beginning to resemble the elephant man. The police officer asked if he could get a statement. I answered, "Of course, but I don't really know what happened. I'm hoping the witnesses can tell me!"

The EMT was trying to look closer at my head; looking up at the officer he addressed him sternly. "Can't you see her head? She's coming with me; you can **not** get a statement from her now! How accurate would it be if you did? He briskly moved me away toward the ambulance. I told him I did not want to leave the lady in the van. "I need to stay with her, she has no one here. I should be with her!" I pleaded. "Can you see how she is?"

"I will check on her soon. She is in good hands. They are taking care of her, right now you need to focus on yourself." Shining a light in my eyes he asks, "Do you know who the president is? What year is it?"

"Is she alive? We couldn't find a pulse."

"She was alive when I saw her, her pulse was weak but she was alive. Now can you tell me who the president is?"

"Truman. Do you think she's going to live?"

Someone else entered the ambulance, another EMT.

"How is the other lady doing?" I asked frantically.

"It doesn't look good" He answered somberly.

His answer took me by surprise. I didn't expect the candor, but did appreciate it. He approached and shined his light in my eyes. "Who's the president? What year is it?"

"It's 2017, the president is Truman. But I don't want to be in here! I want to get back outside and see her!"

"There's nothing you can do, I understand how you feel, but trust me you need to stay here. I really think you need to go to the hospital and get checked out."

"I don't want to do that. I don't have insurance. I'm okay. I'm just worried about her."

"Have you called anyone? Is there anyone we should notify?"

"I called my husband, I think. Oh no! I was meeting my daughter! She has to be wondering where I am I must be late by now!"

"Call her now."

Looking down at my hand, I realized my phone was in it. I didn't remember having it, but was glad it was there. I quickly looked up her name.

"Lai Oshae, I've been in an accident. It's bad, the other lady... I think she might die."

Again this conversation is a blur, I know I started to tell her where I was and realized I had no idea. The paramedic took my phone and talked to her. He must have told her to go to a hospital nearby because we would both end up at Hillcrest Hospital.

"I can't go to the hospital. I don't have insurance. And I won't go anywhere until you let me see her again!"

"You can't see her now. She's being taken care of, she'll be life flighted, no doubt. I really think you should go to the hospital; your head has a nasty bump on it. Who did you say the president is again?"

"Truman, oh (chuckling a little) I mean Trump! I've been saying Truman. That's not because of my head, that's just me. I'm goofy like that sometimes. I know it's Trump- and he's no Truman! I really think I'm okay and I don't have health insurance. Does my auto insurance pay for that?"

"Yes, it will- you really should go, just to be safe. You never know about head trauma." I knew what he was talking about. My mind went back to a time when my family went to a local fair. We watched an exciting motor cross race where one of the bikers crashed. He got up and walked away, but later that night we heard he had died from bleeding on the brain.

"Okay, I guess I'll go. Is it far? How will my husband and daughter know where to go?"

"Don't worry about it, we'll see that they know. You can call them when you arrive and make sure they are on their way. But do you mind if we strap you to a backboard for safety reasons. I know you can walk, but it looks better for us if we take all the precautions."

"Sure. Whatever you want to do."

I had no idea what a backboard even was. I should have, I've seen them on TV, but it didn't register. If I had known what lied ahead, I wouldn't have given permission.

# CHAPTER 2

# DID SOMEONE SAY "TRAUMA UNIT?"

The EMT holds up this hard plastic brace, approximately 10 inches wide, "I'm going to put this around your neck. It's going to be uncomfortable." He placed it around my neck and it hit where my seatbelt had left scrapes and bruises from the impact. Uncomfortable? Yes, definitely!

"How does that feel?" he asks as he tries to gently wrap it around.

"It's fine" I replied. It hurt, but who am I to complain? I most likely just killed someone, and if she lives how much pain and suffering will she go through? And for what? Why? She was just sitting there and I come along slamming her from behind. If I have pain it's deserved. How dare I complain!

"Okay, Lay down on this board, if you could and we will strap you down. It's mostly just to transport you safely. But we should warn you. We are taking you to a trauma unit. It will seem crazy. There will be a lot of doctors and nurses all asking questions. They are trained for intense situations. It will be intense!

That was an understatement!

They went on to place straps around my ankles, legs, pelvis, chest, and head. I have always hated confinement. I don't like belts or bracelets.

Watches, necklaces, and rings even bother me. This was extremely uncomfortable, not only physically but also psychologically. My mind is racing, thinking of how I might get out of this.

"I get car sick, you know. When you start moving, I'm most likely going to throw up."

"We can handle it" smiling at me "Trust me, we've cleaned it up before."

I'm thinking, but I'm not really hurt. I know I'm not. But this is their job; they could get into trouble if they don't strap me down. I don't even need to go to the hospital. I don't need to. But they've been so nice and Delbert and Lai Oshae will go there, they can't come here- the road has been closed off. Okay, okay it will be over soon, just do what you're told. How bad could it be? It's for your own good, after all.

The ambulance ride was nauseating. But, not surprising I always got carsick when I ride in the back. Now I have a severe concussion and strapped to a flat board in a vehicle running stoplights, passing other cars and speeding through turns! Ugh! I felt awful! And the strap over my chest and the neck brace were both digging into the injury sustained by my seatbelt. My arms were strapped down so I couldn't alleviate it if I tried. The stops and turns were jerking my body around, even though I was attached to a board. It seemed like hours, but minutes later we arrived at the nearest hospital with a trauma center.

The trauma center is everything they warned me about and more. There were many, many health professionals running around. Individually running up, shining lights in my eyes "What year is it? Can you tell me who the president is?"

"Trump. 2017." I got this now. I no longer say Truman, I know the drill. My head is much clearer than at the crash sight. But Mary is still foremost on my mind.

"Was the other victim brought here?"

"I don't know. Tell me where it hurts"- shining a light in my eyes still. "You have a nasty bump, does it hurt anywhere else?"

"My right hand hurts, but I'm ok. What about the other lady? When you hear anything can you tell me how she is."

"She must not have been brought here. I haven't heard anything."

Another doctor approaches as that one walks away. "Do you know what year it is?"

"2017. Do you know about the other victim?"

"I haven't heard." The scene is organized chaos.

Everything is very fast paced. People all rushing back and forth. Things are being shouted in the background.

"Auto accident- collision, other victim critical!"

"Wearing seatbelt, airbag did not deploy!"

"Obvious head trauma!"

Wow! This is surreal. It feels like a movie set. I shouldn't be here. This is for people who are really hurt. I wonder why the other lady isn't here. Maybe they did life flight her out of the crash sight. It seems like she should be here. These people could help her. I don't need them, she does.

There are now several nurses all around me. They start to remove my clothes. One is taking off my shirt, while another is pulling off my jeans.

"I'm able to walk, you know. I can remove my clothes, myself."

By the time I get the words out my shirt and jeans have already been pulled off. They are now removing my under garments.

"Man, I'm glad I went on that low carb diet!" I always turn to humor when I feel anxiety.

Seemingly caught off guard by my remark a nurse smiles, "You still have your sense of humor!"

I was trying to make light of tragedy. I always have. Coming from an abusive, tragic childhood I learned to get through hardship any way I could. I know how to disassociate. Although, I must say, part of me *was* actually glad to be 40 pounds lighter in this situation.

Here I lay stark naked as they hook all kinds of wires on me, taped to my chest, my stomach, my arms. There's no way to put a gown on over all this so they attempt to drape one over me.

I've had four kids, two of them a set of high-risk twins. I have been in embarrassing and uncomfortable situations before, but this was pretty extreme. I was very impressed with the professionalism and knew they were all just doing their job, so I just humbled myself and let them do what they had to do.

Multiple times several workers would move me, strapped to the backboard and helpless.

"It's going to feel like you're falling."

Whoa! It felt like some crazy carnival ride. Just about every ride I have ever been on has given me motion sickness. This was no different. Between the concussion, the ambulance ride and this constant flipping my insides are trying to figure ways to get outside. After being humiliated, poked, palpitated, and stuck with many tiny sharp objects it's now time to travel to x- ray. Flying down the hall, still strapped down, the hospital gown refuses to stay across my body. I'm being wheeled by a couple young guys, who though professional, are obviously embarrassed and trying to both move quickly and hold the paper-thin garment across me. It flies to the floor as we round a corner. One of them goes to grab it and once more attempts to throw it over me as the gurney races down the aisle, passing people as they casually make their way through the halls of the hospital. Again I comment on my recent weight loss to try to lighten the mood.

"I'm so sorry" the red-faced young man whispers.

"Hey, I just lost 40 pounds, it's all good!" He smiles and shakes his head, seemingly in disbelief of the circumstances before him. After what must have been a trip around the entire hospital we finally made it to X-ray. Things have calmed down immensely. The medical professionals that work in this area of the hospital are very low key. It almost feels like you've stepped into a totally different world. With the more relaxed environment, in the quiet, my mind again turns to the accident. I wonder how she is. What could've happened? How did I miss a car in front of me? Why didn't I see her? Even if she did have some health problem that caused her to stop there, it still wouldn't explain why I didn't see her. At least I don't remember seeing her. Maybe I did, maybe I just don't remember. I looked down at my hand and realized my phone is in my hand.

"Can I call my husband or my daughter? They're supposed to meet me here."

"Soon. Once the x-rays are done we will get you to a private room. If they arrive before then we will have them wait there for you."

How are they going to know where to go? Lai Oshae is very resourceful. I bet she already knows where to go. She must have talked to her dad too, he would have called.

X-rays took a while, they were very thorough, but finally they were wheeling me back to a room. I can get this neck brace off, get into the gown, and start to feel a little normal. I'm so sick! My head hurts but I can deal with pain. This sick feeling- the world spinning around- is much more difficult.

Back at a room, Lai Oshae is there. My husband, Delbert is on his way. The officer who I first met at the crash site is there also. He introduces himself as he holds out his hand, "Hi, I'm Officer Mack. I'm here to get your statement. Can you tell me what happened?"

"I can try, I'll tell you all I know but I don't really remember. How is the other lady? Is she alive, we couldn't find a pulse."

"I haven't heard. I'll keep you informed. I know she didn't look good. I should tell you, the charges drastically differ if she doesn't pull through."

I could hear the compassion in his voice as he carefully chose his words.

"If she lives, it will probably be a simple traffic citation like "following too closely". But if there's a death everything changes. That is not really up to me."

I understood what he was saying. I was very afraid that she would die, but not because I was afraid of jail or prosecution. I couldn't imagine living with the responsibility of taking a life. The burden of taking someone's mother, grandmother, sister, daughter, best friend. How would I do that? But it's not even about me, there's a family out there whose life will be changed forever.

This was too overwhelming for me to handle right now. My thoughts turned to my eldest son, his father's namesake. He's a police officer. He will understand this better than I do. I'll let him handle this.

"My son is a police officer too, can I call him? Will you talk to him, explain all this?"

"Absolutely! Call him. I will be happy to talk to him!" I dialed my son, briefly mentioned to him that I had been in an accident and the other lady may die.

"Can you talk to the officer on my case? His name is Officer Mack, he wants to talk to you."

What a relief it was to hand that phone over and let them talk. Delbert has always been a leader. He has a "take charge" personality. I don't. I prefer for others to take charge in most cases. And right now my head feels like it's exploding. When I asked about Mary his expression told me all I didn't want to know, I started throwing up. As the night went on, every time we spoke of Mary I would throw up.

After ending the call with my son, Officer Mack continued to talk to me. Delbert had told me not to answer any questions. Lai Oshae was also telling me to stop talking about the accident. When Officer Mack would leave the room, Lai Oshae would say "Quit talking to him, he's trying to lead you into admitting something, just don't talk. You don't remember anything, so that's all you should say."

I understood what she was saying and why she was saying it. I watch crime shows all the time. But this was different. I really wanted to know what happened. I needed to know. Maybe Officer Mack could help me figure it out. He seemed really nice, concerned. He knows my son is a police officer too. They have a brotherhood, a connection, right? I don't care. It doesn't even matter. I will do anything, whatever it takes to find out what happened.

Officer Mack walked back into the room. "So what do you remember?"

"All I remember is traveling down the expressway thinking traffic was moving smoothly, I was making good time...but not speeding. I had set my cruise control to 65 so I wouldn't speed."

"You know the speed limit is only 60 there." He interrupted.

"Well I had braked and was going slower than 65 because I was ready for my exit. I knew I was getting close. I was close to 480, wasn't I?"

"Yeah, a couple miles or so."

"How did she get there? I don't remember seeing her stopped. Did the witnesses see anything? How did this happen?"

"I can tell you what I've seen before. That is a high accident area. With the upcoming exit coming off to the right, the cars in the left lane move on ahead to the front of a slowing right lane to cut in front and exit. That causes the right lane to get slower as it lengthens until it eventually comes to a complete stop. It can happen pretty quickly. There are accidents like yours all the time at rush hour. I have worked this beat for six months and have seen sixteen accidents at that exact spot. When I got the call, I knew exactly where to go!"

A line of traffic? More than one car? How did I miss that? How could I have not seen that?

"How did I miss that? How could I have not seen a whole line of stopped traffic?" My voice was shaky. I felt a pit in my stomach.

The officer pulled out a pen and pad.

"You mentioned you were looking for an exit. Does your gps talk to you when you get close to where you have to do something like that? Maybe you looked at it, if it spoke to you, maybe it took your attention.

"I could have been looking at my gps, I don't remember, but I might have."

"You had mentioned that the accident occurred around 5:30, do you think you may have looked at your clock?"

"I might have looked at my clock, it's possible, but I don't remember. I don't know how I knew what time it was. I really don't know."

"Since you knew you were nearing your exit ramp, do you think you were looking at the exit sign, or perhaps the traffic in the other interstate lanes, you know, because you were thinking about getting off the interstate?"

"I don't know, but that sounds like something I could've been doing. But how could I miss stopped traffic? Wouldn't there be brake lights? Maybe a car had changed lanes in front of me at the last minute? If it blocked my view and then moved over quickly that could make me miss the stopped cars."

"There is an excellent crime scene investigation team going over everything. If her brake lights weren't working we will know. Can I take a look at your phone?"

"Yes, but I'm expecting my husband to call, he should be here soon. He won't know where to go."

"You can hold onto it, we will subpoena phone records anyway."

Officer Mack went on to ask about my family and show me pictures of his son. He stayed at the hospital until I was released. He was thorough and very professional, but somehow made me feel like I made a new friend. That was his job.

# CHAPTER 3

# GOING HOME:
# THE AFTERMATH BEGINS

Delbert arrived and after an hour or so I was released. So relieved to be going home. I was throwing up as a walked out of the hospital, but I did not have health insurance and really wanted to be home. Lai Oshae decided to follow us home and spend the night. She's been very compassionate through this whole thing. I feel so close to her, I don't know if she realizes how important she has been, just having her here.

The next morning I looked in the mirror for the first time. Wow! My head is pretty big! It kind of reminds me of a bag of oranges. You know how they look if they are packed really tight into one of those mesh bags from the grocery store. The skin on my forehead is pulled tight over several lumps, one of which is about the size of an orange, others somewhat smaller. Colors are coming in brighter as the day progresses- purples, blues, reds. And my left eye is just a slit to peer through. My right eye is partially blind due to an old injury, so my vision is very impaired. But as I look at the battered face before me, I wonder how I faired so well. Why is someone out there fighting for her life while I stand here nearly unscathed? Tears are running down my cheeks. As the week progresses more moments will be filled with tears than not. I would not be able to control them.

I did not sleep the night before. I tried to, I knew I had two toddlers to contend with in the morning. The second that I closed my eyes I was back at the crash site, back at Mary's side.

"No pulse! No pulse!!" was screaming in my head. Why, God? Why did this happen? What did I do? How did I do it? Why did God let this happen?

Now it was another day. Go downstairs. Fix breakfast. Try to be normal. Make conversation. You can do this.

My other daughter, who lives an hour away was worried about me and having two kids the same age decided to come and let the cousins play together. It was a beautiful day and one of the perks of coming to grandmas house is that it's a horse farm. They all love to run around and play outside! Not only do they enjoy seeing new foals and petting the horses but there is an array of entertaining outdoor toys for them to play with. Every time I pass a child ride-on toy at a yard sale, I pick it up. Years ago Delbert decided to put in a large concrete area that was used for basketball when our son and daughters took interest in the sport. Now it doubles for a play area for big wheels, tricycles, bikes, battery operated cars, 4-wheelers, and ride-on toys of all kinds. That along with a huge yard connected to it lures the kids outdoors. The grand kids want to play outside every time they come, rain or shine- even in the snow. But today the sun was shining, it was warm and we were definitely spending our day outdoors. Shelby arrived. We set up lawn chairs- Delbert, Lai Oshae, Shelby, and I while the toddlers all played. As we sat around talking, laughing, socializing like we have many times before I tried to convince myself life hadn't changed that much. It would go on just like before. I watched the kids play, broke up their squabbles, helped them up when they fell, wiped away their tears, like I've done many times before. As I wiped their tears, I realized some of my own were falling down my cheeks. I wasn't really even aware of them. The sadness went deep, almost too deep to feel. I kept seeing Mary in my mind's eye, seeing her in her van. I wondered how she was. I called the police department to get an update on her and was told after several calls to not call back; they would let me know if there was any news. That can't be good, I thought. A coma, that would explain no change. She did appear to be in a coma. Patients in comas can stay in an unchanged state for months, even years. I may not know anything for a while.

I need to try to carry on. There are people who depend on me. Things I need to do. Things I need to do! I had already called the church to let them know I couldn't attend worship practice so I don't have to sing tomorrow. But I still need to teach the high school Sunday school class. That's okay. I've already prepared the lesson, I'll be okay to do that. My head really hurts, I'm not sure how well I can stay focused. I hope I can make it through without crying. I think I can, after all it takes a lot to make me cry. I bet I'll be okay tomorrow.

Lai Oshae had mentioned that she needed to get home soon. She needed to call off work because she couldn't find a sitter. Her dad spoke up right away and volunteered to keep the girls like we had planned before the accident. I thought to myself: What? How am I going to take care of them? Whenever I would bend over shooting pain would surge into my head. I know the one year old will need to be picked up period-ically. I will need to bend over somewhat to change diapers. I really do not think this is a good idea. After all Delbert never takes care of the kids, that's all on me.

Lai Oshae looks at me "Could you? I could still work most of the overtime that I planned on taking."

"We have to go back to give your statement sometime this week any-way, Officer Mack said we should be able to get the stuff out of your truck then too." Her dad replied, looking in my direction.

I really did want some of the things that had been in my truck. My kindle that I use to download my practice worship music is in there, and four of my saddles. I wondered if they were okay. I was hoping they weren't damaged, but immediately felt guilty for thinking of such super-ficial things right now.

Wow, I can't even ride now! I have nothing to pull the trailer and no saddles. There you go again being selfish and superficial! Stop thinking like that, that's not important now- not at all!

I had been riding every day that weather permitted. I was training a three year old that I had just started under saddle a few months before. On days when I didn't ride her I took a six year old that I had broke a few years earlier out on trails. There is a really nice trail just a few miles from my home that I like to take them to. It's close enough that it doesn't take all day to go, and short enough to give them low- pressure experience in trailer hauling. Many locals use it for hiking, dog walking, biking, and occasionally we see other horse back riders there. It's a great training trail to let young horses gain exposure to activities they might not otherwise come into contact with. My husband and I had been meeting there in the evenings after work and riding for an hour or so. We often saw deer. We had even seen a bear with her cubs once! It was one of my very favorite things to do and I would miss it.

Again guilt starts to flood my mind. You didn't even want to take your grand kids because it would put a glitch in your riding plans. You are way too obsessed with your horses! Get your priorities straight! Maybe God allowed this to happen so you couldn't ride. It would serve you right if you never replaced your truck or those blasted saddles!

"Of course we'll take them! You go back home, get your work done. I'm fine and we would love to keep them!" I wasn't being dishonest. I really did want them to stay. I wasn't sure how I would manage but I did love having them here.

Throughout the day my mind would drift to Mary, to the sight of her lying lifeless in her front seat. I would quickly try to reset my attention on something else. I can't let my mind go there. I have kids to take care of. If I start thinking about that, about her, I know I will fall apart. I can't afford to do that now. I can't let the kids see me cry. They won't understand. They have seemed unaffected by my face even though I am really looking a lot like the hunchback of Notre Dame. It's amazing what kids will adapt to if we adults just act like everything is normal. So that's what I need to do, at least while they are here. Nighttime will prove to be different altogether.

Shelby and Lai Oshae had each headed home. Delbert had stayed home from work for most of the day to make sure I was okay and help out with the kids. I was in the kitchen cleaning up after dinner when the phone rang. It was a ring tone reserved for numbers I didn't know. I don't normally answer calls from this tone. But nothing is normal right now. I have been answering calls all day from numbers I didn't recognize. People from the church had been calling to reach out and offer to help out in any way they could. I was also expecting a call from the insurance company anytime, and of course, Officer Mack.

# CHAPTER 4

# "I Killed Her!"

O fficer Mack said he would call if there were any news about Mary. I
answered the phone and immediately knew his voice.

"Hello, Mrs. Liller? This is Officer Mack. How are you doing this
evening?"

"Well, you know, not too good but okay I guess."

"Yeah, well um I don't really know how to say this... the victim driving the mini van..."

I knew what he was going to say before he got the words out. My
knees started to buckle. I held onto the kitchen counter so I wouldn't fall.
There was a strange feeling rushing through my body. I felt it whirling up
from my feet, seaming to stop when it got my heart. His voice started to
fade into the background. His words were no longer clear. My head was
throbbing, I felt sick. I knew my life would never be the same. I can't say
how the rest of the conversation went. I simply don't remember anything
that was said after that. Things seemed to be moving in slow motion. I
turned toward the staircase and slowly, almost methodically, I headed
for them. I held onto the railing as I took each step carefully. Tears were
flowing down my cheeks, soaking my shirt. I heard someone crying as I
entered my bedroom door and closed it behind me. I realized that sound
was coming from me. The silent tears that had been streaming down my

face all day had now turned to sobbing. I was now sitting on the floor, moaning, rocking back and forth. The sorrow was over whelming. I was mourning a tragic loss. I wasn't crying for me. There were no thoughts of prosecution, conviction, jail time, or even personal trauma associated with the legacy I now own. My thoughts were for her, the life that was lost. I knew there was a family out there somewhere hurting. A family like mine who no longer have their loved one. There were close friends like the ones who had been calling me all day who would no longer have a confidante. I was mourning in a way that I had never felt before. It over whelmed me, enveloped me, consumed me. I had dealt with death before. I had suffered great loss when my brother who had been my very best friend most of my life was murdered. That news came to me in a phone call as well. But I was able to turn that pain over to God and trust Him with it. I had also lost my dad and an infant son. In every instance I was able to be at peace in the understanding that God controls life and death and that His grace and peace is sufficient for me. But this was different. I did this. I didn't know how. I didn't know why, but I did it. I caused her death. I caused the pain her family and friends were going through. It was my fault and I didn't know how to do this. I felt so alone. So alone.

After some period of time I remembered real life was happening around me. There were a couple little ones downstairs who needed attention. Granddad was doing his best to hold down the fort, but I knew my assistance would be appreciated. So I made my way back downstairs to the family room where they were playing with toys and watching tv. It was nearing their bedtime so we let them watch a program or two and got them wound down before bed. Once they were securely tucked in for the night, Delbert and I headed for our bedroom and turned on the nightly news. As I lie in bed I heard the sounds coming from the set, but it was just noise. The distractions in my head far outweighed anything going on around me. The voices in my head that would plague me in the days ahead had begun their torment.

"Killer. Killer. You're a killer. You were born to kill. This is your legacy. You shouldn't have been born at all."

When you are abused as a child there are certain "truths" that you accept about yourself. You learn them from the abusers. My "truths" had been instilled at a very young age. I had believed that I was a mistake, an accident that no one intended- not even God. I had believed I was not worth anything, no good. I had for years believed there was no good in me. I had struggled for many years feeling like I didn't belong in this world. But through counseling and by God's grace I discovered that His love was for me too. That God was big enough to rescue me. His love was great enough to heal my hurt and restore my soul. I had overcome the voices in my head. I had gained confidence and value through Christ. It had been years since I let the demons of my youth rule my thoughts, but they were back again and they would prove to grow stronger than ever.

We were both tired from the stress of the last 30 hours so we decided to get some sleep. In the dark, the image of Mary in her van was clearer than ever. Now she didn't appear restful at all, now she was completely lifeless. Every time I close my eyes I saw her vividly. I heard the witnesses shouting "No pulse!" But now that's not the only thing I heard. There were other voices too shouting, "You killed her! You killed her!"

I tried to open my eyes to make the images go away, but they were still there.

I decided to get up and try to write a letter to the family of the victim. I went into the study, closed the door behind me and turned on the light. As I sat there, pen in hand I thought of how sorry I really was. I am sorry, very very sorry but how do I put it into words? How do you tell someone that you're sorry for killing their grandmother, their mother, their sister? What do I say? I scribbled down a few things and crumpled the paper up. It's not enough. I don't know how to put into words how I feel. I began to weep. My soul ached for them. I thought about if it were one of my kids. What would anyone be able to say to ease the pain? There's nothing, nothing that can ease that pain. I can't ease their pain, but if it were me, I would want the person to know how special my child was. But I do know that. She is very special. Maybe not as special as she is to them, but I do love her. I actually feel like she's part of me now. Okay. That's where I'll start. I'll let them know how special she is to me. But I don't want them to be burdened if they don't want to forgive me. Heck, I can't forgive myself! Well, I guess I'll write that too. 'I'm not asking for your forgiveness, I haven't forgiven myself.'

I sat up trying to piece something together. It wasn't much, but it was something. I didn't know how I would ever get it to them. I didn't even have a name, but its all I can do right now. This is how it went:

'To the family of the dear lady in the caravan that I hit with my truck on that tragic, tragic day., I want to say how very, very sorry I am. I don't have words, nor could anything I say be of much value to you in these such traumatic circumstances. I just want you to know how sorry I am. I would tell you anything I could if I knew anything myself about what caused this terrible accident. I do not know myself. I've gone over it and over it to try to figure out how I didn't see her in front of me and I am at a total loss. I'm sure your lives are changed forever, as is mine. I don't know why I'm alive and your loved one isn't. It's not fair or right. It's senseless. I am so, so sorry. I can't ask you to forgive me, I can't forgive myself. But please know you will never leave my thoughts neither will that lovely lady. I'm praying for all of you. I truly hope you find peace.'

Tears had soaked the page. I had to rewrite it. There were grammatical errors that went unnoticed and it was thrown together in a hodge podge fashion. But it took hours to write.

The next morning was Sunday. I was scheduled to teach the high school Sunday school class. After Officer Mack called with the devastating news, I had called my dear friend and church secretary to let her know. She, in her wisdom had told me I shouldn't try to teach. I have the personality that once I commit to something I do my very best to see it through. I couldn't sing on the worship team because I had grandkids and couldn't make the practice, but I saw no reason why I shouldn't still teach. As I was getting ready for church I realized how raw my emotions were. I couldn't stop the tears from falling down my face. That wouldn't be fitting for a teacher, so she made the right call. I wouldn't teach. I went through the motions of getting the kids ready. Getting myself ready was easier than normal. When your face looked like mine, no amount of make up will make a difference. My hair didn't matter much either and it hurt to touch my head so I just let it all go, brushing it a little will have to do.

Going to church has been the high point in my life for as long as I can remember. Even in the chaos of my childhood it was a safe haven. There is so much peace in the presence of the Lord. I was excited to be going, maybe putting the tragedy behind me for a couple hours.

We handed the girls off to their designated classrooms, then headed to our class. The people in this class are as close to family as it gets. We were surrounded by love and concern. After a lengthy tear filled prayer time where many brothers and sisters shared their heart felt concerns with our Father, our beloved teacher shared a lesson. I tried to concentrate on the words he was saying. This is God's day. It's set apart to bring glory to Him. I don't want it to be about me. I don't want to be distracted by the events of my life. But this seems to be bigger than my desires. It doesn't seem to matter how hard I try the thoughts of Mary and the crash are foremost in my thoughts. We leave the classroom setting and enter the sanctuary. Many of the members have heard about the accident. There was a prayer chain going around. Few approached and asked what happened to my face. I would calmly answer 'I was in an accident.' I didn't offer more information than I had to. I couldn't say the words without falling apart and this day was not about me. I didn't want the attention, but my bruised and battered face demanded it. The service hadn't started yet and I caught sight of the new youth minister that had just been hired a month or so before. He was such a welcome addition to our body. I loved his passion for God and the teens! We made eye contact and he leaned over to tell me something.

"I just wanted to let you know, the kids all wanted to pray for you when they heard about what happened and you'll never believe who asked to lead it!"

When he told me the name of boy who led prayer, I was very touched. This boy was never serious. He was the class cut-up, always joking. I had never been able to get a straight answer from him. I knew how special this was for him to do.

The music began to play. I knew the songs well, I had practiced all week. Even though I had sang each one many times through, it felt as though I was singing them for the first time. As we sang the words "there's no place I would rather be than here in Your love, here in Your love" it had never meant more to me. There was truly no place I would rather be than in church, worshipping God. As tears ran, I thought to myself if I could stay here, never leave, I would be okay. I could do this if I could just stay here.

I got through the day Sunday, playing with the kids -going through the motions of daily normal life. Throughout the day voices were echoing in my head. I recognized them. They were very familiar to me and took me back to a time that I had long since put behind me- at least I thought I had. Those voices were now closing in, getting louder and louder.

"I told you shouldn't have been born."

"This is what I tried to tell you! You were never supposed to be here and now we know why- you were destined for something like this!"

"You have tried your entire life to do 'good', but this is really who you are."

"This is your legacy- any good that you thought you have done is just a lie anyway. This is who you were born to be- a killer! Killer!! KILLER!!"

My childhood was inundated with chaos. Yelling and screaming were the norm. Degrading and humiliating remarks were way more common than pleasantries. To say that my family was dysfunctional is like saying lava is a little warm. When a child grows up with constant belittling and berating, it sticks with them. My parents grew up in their own unfor- tunate situations and it managed to carry into our family. The children growing up in that household were very damaged. My brother and I may have showed more outward signs of that damage than the other siblings. An example of this is up until the age of 13, I rocked back and forth and sang to myself –not only when I was alone but often when surrounded by people. My brother sucked his thumb until nearly into his teen years. I remember a conversation that he and I had when I turned 12 and he was 10. Tired of the ridicule from school bullies and the drama on the school bus, I approached him one day with a game plan. I told him that it was time for both of us to learn how to be 'normal'. We had grown extremely close through the years defending and depending on each other. We had a unique bond and understood each other. I knew why he 'needed' his thumb, and he related to why I got lost in my own world so much that I wouldn't even notice the stares from onlookers. But we both decided to keep an eye on each other and let the other one know if they were slipping into the vices that for years helped keep us sane.

I struggled through my teen years fighting the urge to slide back into the false security that I got while distancing myself from the outside world. I worked hard at coming out of the protective shell that I had carefully built around myself. The child that I thought I had left behind was beginning to resurface and I didn't like her.

During the day these resounding declarations were destructive, at night they were crippling. Attempting to sleep had become futile, closing my eyes nearly unbearable. In the dark, the atmosphere around me would transform from a peaceful, quiet country farmhouse to the frantic, crazed expressway that I had inadvertently turned into a crime scene. I would find myself curled up on the bathroom floor, swaying to and fro reverting back to the child-like state that had paralyzed me so many years before. Flashbacks of times spent hiding in a closet when the world became too harsh to bear, now began to penetrate my identity. I could feel the person who had climbed out of that world of despair slipping away and it scared me. I prayed.

"Oh, God why did this happen, how did this happen? I'm so sorry. What did I do? Why did you let me be born? I know you ordain life, why did you allow me to live long enough to do this?"

My mind went back to several events that could have ended my life; events that I had attributed to the grace of God for sparing me. I had been in a roll over accident in my twenties that rendered the vehicle I was in mangled beyond recognition. I appeared from the carnage unharmed. I had contemplated suicide many times as a youth, but never followed through. Even the passion of my life- training horses- had left me with several concussions. I now wondered why God had chose to extend my life only to bring me to the place where I would destroy others.

Monday morning came. If I had slept at all, it was mere minutes fragmented here and there. My daughter, Shelby had called informing me of her plans to visit again on that day. She was just here on Saturday and living an hour away, weekly visits were rare. I knew she was concerned. It would be good to see her again and the cousins could all play once more. They would like that. Delbert can go to work for a little while. He never stays home on weekdays but I knew he would feel the need to stay with me if no one else was here.

She got here in the morning and we sat in the family room as the children played and watched tv. I was talking to her about the possibility of jail time. I told her I wasn't concerned at all and actually wanted to go. The feelings of guilt were so immense that I would welcome some sort of retribution. I noticed as I went on, she was eerily quiet. After several minutes, I changed the subject to more superficial conversation about the playing children before us. The afternoon took us outside once again. Something disturbing was happening. I watched as the kids played, bantering back and forth, lacking social skills but engaging as kids do. There is a lot of humor in the dynamics between toddlers. They are extremely entertaining. Well, usually. However, there was a change in me that had distorted my world so much that I found no pleasure in anything anymore. I felt an all-encompassing darkness when I looked at my grandchildren. New personal 'truths' were infiltrating my thoughts.

'You took someone's grandmother away, how dare you enjoy yours.'

The same thing would happen when I looked at my kids:

'There are kids out there right now without a mother because of you- you have absolutely no right to have yours around you!'

Around lunchtime my youngest son appears outside. My husband had built a mini apartment above our garage. It's primitive but has everything needed to sustain a person. There is a bedroom with Internet and TV, a kitchenette with a washer and dryer. Many people have resided there when in need of temporary housing; it has served its purpose well. Now Dakota at 21 years old was trying to save money to go to college, so these living arrangements suited him well. And as for me I thoroughly enjoyed having him close.

"Look at your face!" he said with a grin. He hadn't really seen me since the accident, and even if he had my face took on a new quality everyday. Colors would brighten, and then darken. Bumps would seem to appear and disappear daily. Edema is an interesting thing; being fluid-like it morphs into differing shapes as the healing progresses. At this stage my forehead had enlarged to a small grapefruit growth and the colors were at their brightest.

Dakota stayed outside with us for an hour or two, engaging in casual conversation. This would be one of the few times I would see him over the course of the next couple of weeks. I knew why. Dakota was my 'worrier'. One morning when he was in grade school, as he was getting ready to head out for the day I started having extreme nausea. I told him he needed to finish getting ready and make sure he met the bus on time, but I had to go lay down because I wasn't feeling well. He was a responsible little guy and got himself out the door and to school. But once there, concern for my welfare wouldn't allow him to concentrate on the activities at hand. So he went to the teacher and told her he was worried about his mother and the way he left her. She promptly allowed him to call me. Once he heard that my stomach issues had been resolved only then could he carry on with the events of the day. And now at this stage of his life he had his own emotional baggage to deal with. Only a few short months before thoughts of suicide led him to my room at two o'clock in the morning. Plagued by anxiety about his future and relationships, his despair and fragile emotional state left him teetering on the edge. He was aware of his vulnerability and kept himself distanced from things that might lead him back into emotional turmoil.

Dakota left for work, Shelby and her kids went home. Shortly after Shelby had returned home I received a text.

'Mom, you know I don't do well with emotional things. I couldn't say this to your face without falling apart, so I waited until now. I don't want you to go to jail. When you were talking about it I was ready to cry, but held back. Jails are there for a reason, for people who do bad things intentionally. You are a really good person- you don't belong in jail.'

This text made me cry. Shelby is my emotional child. She wears her heart on her sleeve. She feels everything very deeply. She was trying to stay strong for me, but this was killing her inside. She has always been incredibly devoted to her mom. I started thinking about how much all of this was affecting everyone around me. It wasn't just me who would pay for this tragedy, my loved ones were hurting now too and once more I was the reason for their pain.

I got a call in the afternoon from my auto insurance carrier. They were calling to get a more detailed account of the accident. I had spoken with them once before, but now there was a death and they had switched me to a different department more equipped to deal with what that would entail. As the person went over the facts, as they understood them, he asked me an alarming question.

"Did you know you hit another vehicle?"

"I what? What do you mean, another vehicle?"

"Yeah, I have the police report in front of me. You hit a box truck!"

"Are you sure?" I asked, thinking he was reviewing the wrong case.

"I'm sure. It says here your headlight was found lodged in his bumper."

"Oh, no! Was there anyone else hurt? How can that be? How did I not see that truck? That had to be in front of me when my truck stopped. Why don't I remember that?"

The strangest part about this memory lapse is Officer Mack had told me this in the hospital, Somehow I had repressed that memory altogether.

"No one was hurt in that vehicle. There was only minimal damage."

"A small sense of relief came over me." When we had finished the information exchange and I had hung up the phone, emotions once again

32

surged thru me. The realization that more people could've been harmed or even killed in this collision hit me hard. Did God spare me from something far worse? I'm not sure how I can live with this, but how much worse to have to live with another family in pain! And what if my grandkids would have been in the truck? What if I would have killed one of them, devastating one of my children in the process? This could be worse. It's bad, very bad – but it definitely could be worse!

Later that day, a young lady that I had mentored called just to check up on me. We had a very good relationship she was like a daughter to me, and she knew it. She had married right out of high school and as many young wives do, she had struggled with insecurities that had plagued me in my younger days. We had bonded and she would share everything with me. I was hoping she could learn from my experience and deal with hers better than I did mine. So when she called, I was delighted to hear from her. She had taken on a Spiritual leader role of sorts.

"I've been praying for you, I wanted you to know that, and I've been asking God to guide me and give me wisdom to help you get thru this."

I was deeply moved. I felt both honored and proud. She had come such a long way in her spiritual walk. It was ironic in a way. I had spent years mentoring her spiritually, and she is ready to give some back. She didn't know how far back I had slid on my walk in the past few days. She knew I was hurting, but no one but my husband knew of the child like regression that would take place in me when the world around grew silent. She went on:

"I feel God leading me to tell you to call your sister. Have you told her what happened yet?"

My sister! No, I hadn't. I hadn't really told anyone. Delbert had called the church right away, before he even got to the hospital, so many people knew. When something like that gets put on the prayer chain, it makes it through the church pretty quickly. But none of our family lived around us, so they attended different churches. I hadn't notified any of my family, outside of our sons and daughters. My sister, Lisa and I had been very close thru the years. There were many where I would have considered her my best friend. Through the years living across states and growing families with the commitments they bring has caused us to drift apart. We still talk on the phone, not as often as we should, but when we do, it's as if time has stood still. We have an unbreakable bond.

"I haven't, but I guess I should. I haven't thought to at all, but you're right- I should." I thought to myself if this would've happened to her, I definitely would want to know!

"Okay, I'll call her. And thank you, thanks for praying, and thanks for calling." We got off the phone and I put a call into my sister. I got her voice mail.

"Lisa, something really bad has happened. I've been in an accident. Call me when you can."

It's common to get her voice mail. She, like me is very busy with life. She runs several specialty shops in the malls in her area. She also has been blessed with many grandchildren to utilize both time and attention.

It wasn't long and I got a call back from her.

"What happened? Tell me."

I went on to explain the details of the accident. It was very hard to retell the events of that tragic evening. Somehow, I managed to relay it and there was a period of silence.

"That's terrible! I'm so sorry! While you were talking, I was thinking about how that easily could have been me!"

When she said that, when I heard those words, I thought 'it could have been her!' It really could've been!

My sister is an intelligent, resourceful, creative person. But she is also very easily distracted. I had been a passenger in her car many times when I kissed the ground once we got to our destination! I had seen her veer across center lanes while focusing attention somewhere else more than once. I remember on one occasion, she cheerfully waved, as if to say 'Hello', to an on-coming car as he honks his horn. He gestures, not a nice gesture mind you, the kind drivers make when they have narrowly missed clipping an on coming vehicle.

"People are always so friendly! Always waving and honking!" Lisa had stated with delight- oblivious of the road-rage the on coming driver had portrayed (his gesture was not meant as a greeting- not at all!)

Now, after telling her of my misfortune, Lisa continued, "I have rear ended cars a couple times, I've just been lucky enough to have not been traveling very fast when I hit them."

We went on to talk about family and her stores. She was beaming with news of how God had been working in her life, little miracles that could only be God showing up each day. It was thrilling to hear her boast of God's wonder! Her faith had taken on a new dimension over the past few years. It was always exciting to hear her faith soar as He reveals Himself in the events in her life. When we ended that call I felt better. I was still along way from being whole, but God had revealed something thru Lisa that I had been missing. My accident could've happened to a good person. If it would have been Lisa telling me the details of that night - that she struck an innocent victim just sitting in traffic- I would've felt compassion, not rage. I would've known she didn't have malicious intent. I would have wanted to hold her, not hurt her. God had given me a message thru my sister. It was a message that I wasn't quite ready to accept in my heart, but my head received it and acknowledged it, at least for a moment.

# CHAPTER 5

# THE POLICE DEPARTMENT-
# I'M GUILTY!

My son, Del and his family arrived on Tuesday. He was concerned about the statement that I was to make the next morning to the police detective. He knew my state of mind. I had discussed with all my children my desire to ease the family's burden in any way possible, even if that meant jail time. It was my intention to tell the detective in the morning that if it would help the family move on, I would welcome jail time. My son did not want me to make such a statement to the officers. He was determined to stop me.

Wednesday morning arrived. My daughter-in-law, Paige, decided to stay at our house with the kids and visit with her mom, Marcy, who lived closer to us than to them. They had agreed ahead of time to go shopping locally while we were away. So my husband, Lai Oshae's kids, my son Del and his two-year-old son Delbert the fourth all headed to the police station. Delbert the fourth insisted on coming, he's very attached to his grand dad who adores him right back. We had arranged to meet Lai Oshae to exchange the kids. She wanted to go along with us to the station. She and her brother had the same thought process. They were both concerned about my statement. They both knew me well. They knew my concern for the family so out weighed any thoughts of my own welfare that there was potential for self-harm. My children had tried to get me to hire an attorney. There was no way that was going to happen. I wanted justice, as much as they did, but I didn't know what justice was because I had no memory and the responsibility for the accident did fall to me. More than anything I wanted answers. Getting an attorney seemed counter-productive to that end.

We all walked in to the lobby of the department, but only I was allowed to go back in with the detective and Officer Mack. Officer Mack was a relatively young patrolman, looked the part - tough and rugged - but as it turned out he must have had a sentimental side, as well. He had the foresight to save my crumpled "Jesus" license plate from my truck. This plate would turn out to mean a lot to me in the days that followed. Detective Curry introduced himself. He struck me as being young for a detective. I found out later he was around 50 he just looked very young. We exchanged pleasantries, making light conversation for a minute or so to ease the tension. This was difficult for me and somehow, I felt, may have been unsettling for him as well. A life was lost and I'm sure that is never easy to deal with, even for law enforcement. He had to be professional and handle an emotional situation without emotion- even while those around him fall apart.

He sat across from me scanning through my file.

"I see here you were looking at your gps, checking the clock, looking for exit signs?"

Officer Mack spoke up. "No, no, She didn't say she was doing all those things. We were speculating. She doesn't remember what happened."

It was a relief to hear Officer Mack speak up for me. I'm aware that a lot of people would be nervous, maybe even afraid in this situation. I was not at all. Perhaps, because I respect the authoritive nature of law enforcement or it may be simply because the worst had already happened. A precious life had been taken, how could it get worse than that? This to me was a step toward a sense of resolution, not only for Mary's family, but for mine as well.

"I'll tell you anything I can, but I don't remember much. I was hoping the witnesses had seen something, or maybe the crime scene investigators discovered something?"

They didn't really answer me. I thought to myself 'this is a criminal case, they can't- or won't tell me what they have discovered.'

I told the detective jail time didn't worry me.

"If it would help the family move forward, you know gain closure, I want to go. I have heard cases where people can't move forward in their grief because the person responsible hadn't been held accountable. I don't want that to happen."

The detective looked at me with a combination of disbelief and compassion.

"I have been doing this job for a long time. I deal with a lot of people who need to be in jail. You're not one of them! I definitely don't want to see one of them let out to make room for you."

The questioning procedure went on for probably an hour or so. I asked again about the family as I was walking out.

"We're not really permitted to discuss that with you. I would like you to know they are not holding this against you, that's all we can really tell you."

It was important to hear that. It didn't take away the guilt or pain, but there was a tinge of peace when I thought they had forgiven me, not as much for me but because forgiveness is a sign of moving forward in times of grief. Losing my brother years before to murder, I knew how important forgiving could be to a person's quality of life.

I had handed the detective the apology letter that I had written and asked about getting it to the family. I was told it wouldn't happen any time soon. They would send it out, but the charges had to be answered first so it could be a couple months.

That was hard to hear. I wanted more than anything else at this point to tell the family that I was sorry. I wanted to let them know Mary's life was vitally important to me. It was looking more and more like this was never going to happen.

# CHAPTER 6

# HER NAME WAS MARY

We said our good-byes to Lai Oshae and her kids and journeyed back to our home. As we entered our house that evening, exhausted from the stresses of the day, Paige and her mom had a pleasant surprise waiting for us. They had decided that I needed a nutritious solid meal. So her mother purchased all the ingredients to prepare a favorite of mine- Mexican fajitas. Paige prepared a delicious meal for all of us to enjoy. Previously that week, I had received beautiful flowers from Marcy, as well. The concern and love she had shown was truly appreciated in the midst of such turmoil. Delbert and his family went back home that evening as well. With the house quiet, I decided to call my insurance adjuster one more time to try to get a name. Once again I was told they could not release it, but they had also informed me that new documents had been placed online for me to view. Evening turned into another sleepless night. The bed, which had once been a place of serenity and refuge, was now one of torment. Rather than toss and turn in anguish, I opted to get up and see what the insurance company had ready for me to view. As I looked through the paperwork a name caught my eye! There it was! An oversight, perhaps. Divine intervention was more likely. Her name was Mary Schlabach. 'That's unusual', I thought. 'I bet I can find her online somewhere.' Sure enough within seconds, I had come across her obituary.

The name that had eluded me for days was now before me with a smiling face above it! 'That's her!' I would know her anywhere. She looked different than when I saw her, but it was her. There was so much life in her face, so much joy. I had taken that life away. The excitement that came over me on finding her was now being replaced by overwhelming grief. The crash site filled my mind- the panic, the despair. My heart started to race, tears began to saturate my shirt. This was hard, maybe the hardest thing I've ever been through, but I found her! I immediately pasted the obituary on my face book page. Is this strange? Will everyone think it's morbid? It's the only picture I have and I want her on my page with the rest of my family.

The picture I had found attached to her name was from her obituary on a funeral home website. It had family listed as well as a brief description of the life before the tragedy. I felt closer to her. I felt the closest thing to joy that I had felt since this happened.

'I would've really liked her; we would've been close in a different world. Why couldn't our paths have crossed a different way? I felt the tinge of fleeting happiness leaving my body as reality once again swept over me. 'She's not your long lost best friend- you killed her! She was a special person, a Godly lady, and she no longer fills this world with the love and service that she once did- because of you!'

Learning about Mary was bittersweet, but I wouldn't have gone without knowing more about her for anything. I studied the information on that page. I read the names of her family over and over until they were as familiar as my own. As it turns out, Mary had never been married, no biological kids. The information did have "adopted family" listed, however. There were two names there. It also showed two brothers and a sister but her parents had already passed on. There was a little relief in reading this. I'm sure she was well loved and will be deeply missed, but I had struggled all week thinking of how my children and grand children would accept the news of my death. I knew that if I would get called home right now it would be most difficult for them, and of course, my husband.

I had not been intimate with my husband since the accident. This was not the norm for us. We were very close. We had been married twenty-seven years and had had our share of rough patches, but were at a very strong place in our relationship. I couldn't imagine life without him, and I knew he felt the same. This catastrophe, though, had the potential to change all that. My emotions were shutting down. I was putting up the all-familiar wall that I had torn down years before. The wall that kept me from feeling things that were too hard to feel. I didn't deserve to love and be loved with what I had done to another family. I knew shutting down was not fair to the others in my life. I knew it was not the right way to handle this pain and hardship, but it was what was familiar to me and what my body was doing- like it or not. I didn't know if I had the ability to stop what was happening inside me. I hadn't had that fortitude in the past- I knew that. Seeing that Mary wasn't married might allow some of the guilt I felt when I lay beside my husband to dissipate – I was hopeful.

The viewings and funeral were being held at a Methodist church. This was comforting to me as well. All indications were that Mary was a Christian. She was with God. For decades I have had a strong desire to go home to be with my heavenly Father and start the next, more important, chapter of my life. Christians have a different perspective on death. Our faith in the grace of God leads to a hope for something better yet to come. Death is not the end of something, but the beginning of a new exciting life without the pains and burdens that this one holds. The service for Mary was referred to as a 'celebration of life'. Celebrating Mary's life, the one she lived here and the promised one she's embarking on now, would be a welcome change to what I had been doing.

The memorial site was very well done. It had a page designated for condolences and messages to the family. This would be a way to express my remorse to the family. I was aware of the dangers of posting a message on this board. It was a site designed for family of the victim. Its possible, perhaps probable, that any message from me would not be welcome. In the very least, I am a reminder of the horrific events that took Mary's life. How could I be sure my words wouldn't cause more harm? I couldn't. However if there's a chance they could help precipitate healing, wasn't it worth the risk? I wasn't sure. I decided to call a couple of close Christian friends and ask them to pray about it, and of course I prayed. I remembered what I had learned at the police department. The family didn't hold anything against me. That's what he said. But I knew he didn't speak to all family members. He couldn't have. Everyone deals with death differently. Grief takes on many forms, often anger. The decision was not an easy one, but I decided to post an apology. It read:

"I hope this isn't out of turn. I just had to reach out to tell you how sorry I am. I am the driver who hit Mary. I was with her that evening and she will always be in my heart. I prayed over her. I am so so sorry. She was beautiful. My prayers are with all of you. Words cannot express my sorrow. I can't ask you to forgive me, I can't forgive myself. Mary is now a very significant part of my life and I will never forget her. God bless you all and I pray you find peace."

Well, there it was. It was out there now. Emotion flowed as I penned these words. Sorry, I really was. The words haven't been created to express how much. Will they understand the bond I now felt for their loved one? Will this offend someone? Do I have a right to such a connection? It couldn't possibly match how they feel anyway. Will they think I am callous to the upheaval I have caused; to the raw emotion they are now faced with everyday? I know that pain all too well. Losing my brother left a huge hole in my life. To think that I contributed to someone else feeling that emptiness is almost too unbearable a burden to carry.

As I sat looking at my expression of sorrow before me, I contemplated deleting it. I wasn't even sure if I could. But I decided to leave it and continue to pray for God's will to be done.

Thursday morning had arrived. It would be the first day without children to keep me distracted. My nights had been so difficult that Delbert was worried about leaving me alone. He had committed to do some work on the church parsonage, so we both decided it best that I go along. He could drop me off at the church where I could talk to the minister and maybe get some help dealing with the trauma I had been going thru. I called ahead to make sure he had time and we headed to the church.

I went through some of the emotions that had been plaguing me. He listened, very compassionately. When I had finished he asked me a couple questions.

"What would you say to someone who was involved in an accident like yours? Would you feel like they should be condemning themselves like you are doing? This would be different if you would have been drinking, but even then, wouldn't you tell someone else that they need to forgive themselves? Wouldn't you have them repent and ask God for forgiveness? You are sorry, very sorry. You have repented of any wrongdoing you may have done, do you believe God has forgiven you? Wouldn't He forgive someone else? I think you know the answer, you just need to accept it, accept forgiveness and forgive yourself."

I knew he was right.

"I know you're right. I know all the right things to say. I know what I would say to others in my shoes. I just don't know how to apply it to myself. I'm trying it's just not working."

"Well, let me ask you this? How many times a day would you say that you rely on God's grace?"

"I'm not sure what you mean."

"I think you are probably a lot like me in this respect. We spend our days trying to figure out what needs to be done to accomplish God's will, instead of allowing God to work. Sometimes there are things that we are expected to do and sometimes we are meant to step back and let God's grace cover us. There are times when He doesn't expect us to take action but our action is in letting Him work while we wait by faith. This is one of those times for you. There is nothing you can do, you have already proven that to yourself. Maybe someday you will be able to apologize to them, or somehow make amends, but right now, let grace cover you."

He was right. I knew he was. I was and am a control freak. I like to micro manage everything. I also knew that God would not want me to live a joyless life. He has commanded us to have joy in all circumstances. I had already been writhing with guilt over losing all my joy. The scripture of 'joy in all circumstances' had haunted me. How could I find joy in this?

I was able to have joy in death before because I believe God is in control of life and death. As creator it's ultimately His call to make. 'The Lord gives and the Lord takes away'. I get that concept. But this was different than any death I had dealt with before. I felt so responsible that I had managed to take God out of this life and death equation.

I went home ready to take the much-respected advice. But after returning home it took less than an hour for me to go back to the funeral parlor website and resume my study of the obituary and condolence pages. I was hoping with all I had in me that a family member might have read my message and replied, but so far- nothing. I continued to look at it all day, praying, hoping... and then, finally hours later... there it was! Someone had responded!

Her name was Minerva. I recognized it. She was one of the "adopted" family. A daughter? Her message was incredibly generous and heartfelt. As tears fell, I read:

"Greetings! Tracy Liller, we are the family of Mary and we are really glad that you reached out to us. We have been praying for you and were longing to make contact but the police won't give us information til the investigation is complete. We can not imagine what you are going through and we want you to know we care deeply and we do not hold anything against you. We will miss Mary tremendously but God in His sovereign plan chose to take Mary home that day. His ways are higher than we can ever imagine. Please try to not be too hard on yourself and our family would like to meet up with you if possible. Blessings and grace to you."

Grace. She was extending grace to me. It felt amazing, freeing. I was humbled. It was so undeserved, but that's what grace is- undeserved. She didn't know me, but I had been on her mind and in her prayers. Her heart went out to me? To me? It was my fault that her world was changed forever; my fault that her heart ached, yet she worried about how I was.

'We', she said 'we' have been praying, 'we' care deeply. I wondered who - Mary's sister? Her brothers? I read the reply over and over again. It was the closest thing I had to Mary. The closest I had come to a sense of peace. God had sent Minerva to me. I knew it then, but I had no idea how important she would be to me in the days to come.

I had read Minerva's response in the evening, a little before 5:00. As the night unfolded I couldn't stop thinking about meeting the family. She said they all wanted to meet me. I wondered if she was just being polite, or if they sincerely wanted to meet me. Why would they? I knew why I wanted to meet them so badly. They were my link to Mary, the only link I had. They could help me know her. I had a hole inside me that I was convinced needed to be filled with Mary's life. We had intersected that night in such a way that left me hollow inside. It was unfinished. I didn't want it to end that way. It was like leaving a movie before the 'happily ever after'. I needed a happily ever after ending. Okay, so I wasn't going to get that, but if I could know more about the life she lived I could replace the only thoughts of her I had with happier ones- at least I could do that.

Was there a way to meet them? I had studied the memorial page and knew when all the services were being held. I also had gotten an address and figured out they were taking place three hours away from me. Going to a viewing was impossible. But there was a funeral in the morning.

'Are you crazy? The funeral? Her family could not possibly want you at the funeral! That's a time for them to mourn, they don't need you adding to their sorrow by showing up and reminding them of the catastrophe that took her from them.'

I had already stepped in where I didn't belong, invading their family unit when I got on the condolence page in the first place. Just because they were gracious, forgiving people- that didn't give me liberties to invade further. I tried to put that notion out of my mind. It wasn't leaving. I remembered once again the wise words of my minister.

'Don't get your hands in there and mess this up. God has allowed you to hear that they forgive you. Let that be enough. Let God's grace cover you'

I called a couple people and asked them to pray about this.

"I want to go to the funeral. I want to ask Minerva if she thinks I should. I'm going to post it on the message board of the condolence page.

Ask God to give me the right direction. If I'm not supposed to go, ask God to keep me from going."

Well, people are praying. I asked my husband what he thought. He wasn't a fan of the idea, but said he would do whatever I needed him to do. I hadn't slept in nearly a week, Delbert would've done whatever he could to get his wife back.

The message I sent to Minerva went like this:

'I would love to come to the funeral to pay my respects.. I feel such a strong connection to Mary. If it wouldn't be a burden to anyone there, the very last thing I want to do is cause more pain to your family. Let me know if it would be okay to attend. Thank you so very much for your kindness, it is very undeserved. You must have a great capacity to love, you have already been a blessing to me.'

It was getting late, after 7:00 in the evening. The funeral was to take place at 10:00 am the next morning at a church approximately three hours away. What were the chances of someone seeing my request in time to attend? It really wasn't likely, but I diligently checked the discussion thread as the evening went into the night. Hours went by. I attempted to lie down and try to sleep. I had decided to set my alarm for 5:00 am, just in case someone answered before morning. If I were able to fall asleep, that would allow time to get barn chores done, shower and make the drive. Like all the nights before, sleep once again eluded me. I got up and went to the computer to check for a reply. There was not one. I went back to the obituary, rereading the only real connection I may ever have to Mary. As I was reading the names, something jumped out at me. The names in her family tree were so familiar. I recognized them from the communities surrounding mine. I lived in a rural area; on either side of me was a large collection of Amish families.

'That would explain all the nieces and nephews.' I thought. The obituary had a multitude of offspring coming from the brothers and sister. I had thought it was unusual for all three to have such large families. Now that made sense. I wasn't sure how Mary fit in to the Amish community.

'She was not Amish. I saw her. She was driving a vehicle and dressed in store bought clothes, not the traditional Amish attire. But she had Amish ties. Her family is Amish!'

This revelation, yet another piece in the puzzle of Mary's life that I had been desperately trying to piece together, was encouraging. I had a great respect and appreciation for the Amish culture. I held the discipline in their lifestyle, committing every aspect of their lives to serving God, in high regard. I appreciated that level of devotion and often envied their way of life. Once again, there is a God-fearing Christian connection.

'Mary had to be a devoted follower, all the signs point to that.'

It was so important to me that she knew the Lord. God was showing me all along the way that she was His child. He had her throughout her life and He has her now. I was too self-absorbed to see His truth. God is the creator and sustainer of life. We are His. He is in control-especially of life and death! I still hadn't accepted this truth, not yet. But God would not let me go until I did.

# CHAPTER 7

# WE'RE GOING TO A FUNERAL!

I switched back over to the condolence message board. As I was looking it over, a reply from Minerva appeared, as if by some unearthly, supernatural means. It seemed to just appear from the blank page in front of me. It was late, most people would be in bed, especially someone who had spent the past week preparing for a funeral and welcoming friends and family at the multiple viewings that had taken place over the last several days. Never the less, against all odds, it was there, and she was welcoming me to Mary's life celebration!

'Tracy, you are more than welcome to come to the funeral !! If you come, ask to see me and we will take care of you. We want to be there for you. Be there by 9:15 and we will surround you with love. Just to let you know that it will be a large funeral. Mary had Amish background and lots of relatives and many, many connections and friends. We are expected to have 400 people. This is not to say so you won't stay away but to help you prepare for it. I think it would be very healing and encouraging if you came. You need all the love and support you can get at this time. God bless and good night.'

I quickly responded.

'My husband and I will be there. Thank you so much for your immense kindness.'

I jumped up! I was like a kid on their way to Disneyland! Running around yelling, "We can go! We can go!!! She answered me Delbert, wake up! We can go!"

I startled him from his sleep,

"What? Go where? Who? What are you talking about?"

"The funeral, Mary's funeral! Someone from the family answered my request to go; she said we're welcome! Actually- more than welcome! She wants us there, they want us there!"

His expression was almost one of dismay. The news appeared to have taken him by surprise. He would later tell me, he did not think this was a good idea. Going to her funeral? Really? This has to be stepping beyond what is deemed appropriate social etiquette to say the least. He may have had reservations, but tried not to show anything but acceptance.

For the first time all week, I slept. I still saw the accident when I closed my eyes, but I had a sense of peace. It was not, all-inclusive, but I felt it. It was enough to get a few much-needed hours of sleep. I can't say I slept soundly. I stirred with memories and a degree of turmoil, but I was able to get a little rest.

We got up before 5:00 to get there early. I thought if we got there early enough we could meet the immediate family. I could apologize, answer any questions that I could, and leave them to the more intimate service they had intended. Minerva had told me they wanted me there, but it's likely she was just being nice. I didn't want to invade an already stressful situation. There was also a fear that I would have trouble maintaining composure for a lengthy period of time, especially through a memorial of a life ended by my actions. I didn't want to have any attention on me, not for a second, and taken off Mary where it belonged.

I remained excited on the ride there. As implausible as it sounds, I was not uneasy- not at all. I can't really explain why. I knew I needed something. I felt as though I was close to losing my mind. I felt my sanity slipping away. The guilt was eating me up. I thought maybe if I could just tell her family how sorry I was, maybe I could start the process of healing- for them and for me. Hope, that's what I felt-hope. It felt like my last chance to restore some measure of normalcy to my life. I must admit my motives were somewhat selfish. Of course, I wanted Mary's family restored as well, but I didn't know how my presence would affect them. I had an overwhelming desire to know more about Mary. I felt a kinship that I couldn't explain. It was as if I did know her already, but couldn't remember anything about her. It left me feeling incomplete, fragmented. There seemed to be so much to gain from going to this service, I didn't allow myself to consider the downside.

The route we had to take took us right by the crash site. I guess the memory loss that I suffered went deep because it might as well have been any other strip of road. My husband and I were both concerned about what affect driving thru that area would have on me mentally, but the more we neared the area, the less familiar it was. The mind is a magnificent thing. It was protecting me from unimaginable heartache and stress. God has truly created our bodies with amazing resilience.

We approached the church. There were groups of people standing outside all around the building. The men were mostly clad in black suits with black hats; the women wore black dresses below their knees and predominately white hair bonnets. They were Amish. There were a few people dressed in more secular attire. As we entered the building, I felt a pit develop in my stomach. Many, many Amish people lined the walls of the entryway. To our right was a receiving line with a small line of loved ones gathering. We had arrived almost an hour ahead as requested, but there was already probably two hundred people there. I saw Minerva almost instantly. I recognized her from face book. I had looked up her profile before I asked to come. I knew from reading her posts that she had a very strong faith, which contributed to my decision to ask. Knowing she was a fellow sister in Christ emboldened me to take this step, now I was questioning that judgment call. The men and women grouped along the walls were very reserved. Some were talking quietly but no one made eye contact with me. They seemed to all have their heads down. Most stood with their hands folded in front of them. Someone noticed me walk in. I still had a large bump on my head. I was swollen and bruised, making it obvious to those looking for my arrival. She quickly made Minerva aware of my presence. Minerva left the duty of greeting Mary's friends and family to welcome me.

Her arms were open as she approached. I opened mine and we tearfully embraced.

"I'm so, so sorry! So, so sorry!"

"Don't be sorry! God had a plan; you don't need to be sorry. I'm so very glad you came!"

As she spoke, the knot in my stomach started to fade. She was very sincere and I was equally humbled by her acceptance and out pouring of love. Her voice soon took on a tone of regret.

"I have to get back to the line. I'm sorry we don't have more time, I really want to talk to you."

She called to a lovely lady across the room. She was a striking presence, dressed in a long, flowing skirt and wide brimmed hat.

"Robin, this is Tracy. She is the lady involved in the accident with Mary."

Robin, as it turned out was the very best person for me to link up with at that moment. She was the wife of a minister who up until recently had pastored the church Mary attended. She and Mary were best friends for many years. She began to tell me everything she could think of about Mary.

"Mary and I sat right over there every Sunday." She stated with a joyous expression across her face as she pointed to a pew on the right side of the church, just a couple rows from the front. "I remember the first time she walked thru these doors. She was wearing her Amish dress and cap, you know the whole deal. She actually attended here for a while in traditional Amish dress. Mary was such a devoted Christian. She knew her bible better than anyone I've ever known. Bible study was a passion of hers. She wanted everyone she knew to experience the connection to God that you get thru reading His Word. She was involved and led many Bible studies herself."

If I had any uneasiness being there, Robin was the one to relieve it.

The way she described Mary, I could visualize her. She went on to describe Mary as "no nonsense". She was the kind of person that spoke her mind.

"We got along well, we were so alike in that way. I tell it like it is, just like Mary did. She could talk to me when she wanted to just vent, because I understood it was just her way. She couldn't offend me and I couldn't offend her. I'm going to miss that."

The best way for me to describe Robin is jubilant. As she went on about everything that came to her mind to help me know Mary, she lit up. There were no tears. She told me she knew where Mary is now and there is no reason for sorrow.

"Mary wanted to go home to be with her Father. She was ready to go. She had expressed to me on more than one occasion her desire to 'go home'. She was getting more and more tired, she felt her body was wearing out. She had said that she did not wish to be a burden on anyone, and the way she was feeling, she feared that she would. The community she lived in believes strongly in looking after each other, that responsibility would generally fall to a biological child. But Mary had no biological children and she sure didn't want to burden her nieces or nephews! She was praying for God to take her before that was an issue. She had a strong relationship with Jesus Christ. She is where she wants to be. I can't be sad for Mary, she is in glory walking the streets of gold!"

Robin went on to tell me about Mary's love of children and special gift for helping those with special needs.

"God had blessed Mary with a heart for people who needed extra help learning ways to function better in this world. Autistic kids were especially dear to her. She had been educated in innovative ways to help them live more productive lives." I later learned of the extent that this desire took her. While Mary was still living as a practicing Amish, she had journeyed from Ohio to Utah to educate herself in a special study that would enable her to teach these kids to tap into areas of the brain that would assist in their development. The technique she learned is newly discovered, and though demands tremendous time and effort has proven to be very beneficial for the patient.

Robin went on to tell me that Mary loved to drive. She said one of the things Mary loved to do was transport members of the Amish community. It was not uncommon for her to put 70,000 miles on her van in a year. Her connection to the Methodist church and her beloved family ties created a desire to bring the two cultures together. She was working with both to try to join the two in home Bible studies. There were so many people being positively affected through Mary's labors! As the stories unfolded before me, I couldn't help but have mixed emotions. It was a comfort to know that by the grace of God when this life on earth has ended those who give their lives to Him are alive and in the presence of our Lord and Savior, but the sense that there is less good in this world because she is not here now was hitting me hard.

# CHAPTER 8

# WHAT HAVE I DONE NOW?

We had sat and talked for around a half hour or so and I realized the church was starting to fill up. The sanctuary was set up with three sections of pews. Robin, Delbert and I had sat in the front center-a section reserved for immediate family, Minerva had told Robin to have us sit there with her. It wasn't what I wanted to do, I would've preferred to hide in the back, but the way I saw it I was a guest of Minerva so whatever she asked me to do, I was doing.

As people, mostly Amish started to pack the pews to our right and our left, an elderly gentleman standing in the front of the section we were sitting in, the section reserved for immediate family, made his way over to where Robin, Delbert and I were sitting. This man was dressed in a black suit with a black hat, much like the others around me. He had white hair and beard and donned a stern, stoic expression. In a gruff, authoritative manner he pointed his finger gesturing for us to move from the front row.

"You, Go back!"

He reminded me of a nun in a strict Catholic school striking her students on the fingers for some wrongdoing. He appeared more than irritated. He seemed to me to not want me there at all. I had reacted on impulse- something my preacher had warned me against. Now, as the usher motioned us to move out of the family section, I felt the urge to crawl to the rear, under the pews! My perception at this point may have clouded my judgment. I don't know, maybe my mind created a false analysis of his demeanor. But at that moment I wished I was anywhere but where I was. Minerva's invitation came to mind.

'There is no way Minerva checked with all these people to see if they wanted me to come! I bet she didn't ask the Amish people at all!'

It was close to midnight when she had gotten back to me with the reply. I was aware that the majority of the Amish do not use phones or Internet, how could she have talked to them? I was beginning to feel like I had made a horrible mistake.

Robin was the type of person who wasn't easily intimidated. She stood her ground with the commanding presence facing her.

"No, we're supposed to sit here. Minerva wants us here, she wants *her* here."

Again, he spoke up, using the same forceful gesture as before:

"No! You go back!"

All I wanted to do is 'Go Back'! Go back to the rear of the building. Go back to Pennsylvania. Go back to my bathroom floor and close the door to the harsh realities of this life that I was now forced to live. But, to my dismay, Robin was not about to give in. She did compromise, however.

"We will go back one row, but that's all! Minerva told us to sit here!"

That seemed to satisfy him, or more likely he sensed the adversary before him was not likely to concede. So the three of us got up and entered the pew behind us. As we did this the row of people sitting there proceeded to move to the pew behind them. My feelings of uneasiness grew, as my existence seemed to disturb those around us. I would've bolted out the door if I had an ample opportunity, but as it stood Robin wasn't about to let me leave and from what I just witnessed I didn't wish to defy her. I didn't recognize it at the time, but I realized later my mind and spirit were under attack- a Satan attack. Satan did not want me to stay in that building. He would've loved me to remain in the stagnated existence that the previous week's events had led me to. I'm sure the unproductive, joyless frame of mind and soul that had become my identity pleased him very much.

The seats around us started to fill in with Mary's closest family and friends. Minerva and who I came to know later as her husband sat in the row in front of us. The others around us were unfamiliar. The church had filled to capacity, it looked like over five hundred people to me, my husband and I later estimated maybe four hundred from the Amish community and another hundred or so from Mary's world outside that community. There didn't seem to me to be much inter-mixing between the two groups. I didn't really look behind me, but as I glimpsed the sides of the room, they seemed to consist of the culture Mary grew up in. The people immediately surrounding me seemed to be of a world more akin to mine. I had to wonder if the nature of the accident- being auto related- made those who grew up with Mary more indignant. Knowing the belief system prohibited most from operating vehicles, I worried that the people closest to her may feel I was acting inexcusably as I drove that expressway the evening that our ill-fated collision occurred.

The memorial service was underway and music started to play. The songs, mostly unfamiliar, were still soothing. I had always loved to sing. As a child I would listen to music and sing all day long if given the chance. Music became my refuge from the chaos outside my bedroom door. I had an amazing choir teacher in high school, who had seen potential in my voice and gave me private vocal lessons after school. She spent countless hours with me totally free of charge sharing her gifts of instruction, nurturing the child in me who so much craved that motherly love. As I think of her unselfish devotion to me, I can't help but picture Mary sharing a connection with the children that she had helped thru the years. Many of whom may have needed her loving affirmation as much as I had.

The first song was known to me, however, I hadn't heard it in years; but surprisingly remembered a lot of the words.

'Heavenly sunshine, heavenly sunshine,

Flooding my soul with glory divine.

Heavenly sunshine, heavenly sunshine,

Hallelujah, Jesus is mine!'

As we sang, my imagination soared. I tried to picture Mary with Jesus in all His heavenly glory! What a wonder it would be to one day meet my beloved Savior- and get to see Mary too! I so longed to be there now, to escape the immense pain and sorrow I felt here on this earth. The joy that had eluded me all week would be all consuming in His presence! There would be no guilt there, no self-abasing voices in my head. I imagined being in that place – with Mary.

Once the service started and Robin stopped sharing her memories about Mary, tears began to steadily fall down my cheek. It's impossible to be sorrowful amid the elation exuding from Robin as she regaled the legacy Mary left behind. While engrossed in her tales, I hadn't felt the raw emotion that had overtaken me so often in the days previous. Those emotions were now resurfacing, beyond my control.

'As long as I can stay controlled, it will be alright-just don't lose it!' I thought to myself, aware of the vulnerability within.

The presiding minister read the following scripture:

'Do you not know? Have you not heard? The Lord is the everlasting God, the Creator of the ends of the earth. He will not grow tired or weary, and His understanding no one can fathom. He gives strength to the weary and increases the power of the weak. Even youths grow tired and weary, and young men stumble and fall, but those who hope in the Lord will renew their strength. They will soar on wings like eagles, they will run and not grow weary, they will walk and not be faint.'

Robin had spoken about Mary growing weary. She told me Mary spoke of going home to a place where she would not feel the aches and pains of a body wearing down from years of toil. In Christ, we now share the hope that God has renewed her strength and she is soaring on wings like eagles in the presence of the King!

Hope. Funerals are often filled with this hope. When our loved ones leave this world, we all want to believe we will see each other again and that they are in a better, happier place. The reality is, however that Jesus warns many times that not all will enter the gates of heaven. God is both loving and just. His just nature does not accept sin and selfishness in heaven. He sent His Son to reconcile us to Him, and though we still have a sinful human nature, He gives us His Spirit to dwell in us so we can live a life pleasing to Him. God's grace is the only way to heaven, but there is action on our part as well. God expects obedience, not obedience out of necessity, but because we love Him and choose to serve Him and honor His ways. I'm reminded of the book of 1 John, where John gives us a personal inventory test. 1 John 4:7-8, NIV, says "Everyone who loves has been born of God and knows God. Whoever does not love does not know God because God is love." In verse 20 he takes this a little farther "If anyone says, 'I love God,' yet hates his brother, he is a liar. For anyone who does not love his brother, whom he has seen, cannot love God, whom he has not seen." Why would this be? Because love is a choice. We choose the action of love because by doing so we honor God. When we are truly in a love relationship with God we want to love His children, all of them. John goes on with a more specific relationship test when in chapter 5 verse 2 he says "This is how we know we love the children of God: by loving God and carrying out His commands. This is love for God, to obey His commands." Jesus speaks of this as well when He tells of judgment day. He uses the analogy of separating the sheep from the goats. In this rather lengthy description that I encourage you to read in full in Matthew chapter 25, Jesus shows us that we will indeed be judged by actions that are taken on this earth. These are actions that reflect the love we have for both God and His creation. Jesus says many will come to Him calling "Lord, Lord" as if they know Him, but He will discard those who did not serve here on earth. Jesus gives us a visual image of that day when He comes back with all the angels to sit in judgment and all the nations will be gathered before Him. Verse 34-36 reads: "Then the King will say to those on His right, "Come you who are blessed by my Father; take your inheritance, the kingdom prepared for you since the creation of the world. For I was hungry and you gave me something to eat, I was thirsty you gave me something to drink, I was a stranger and you invited me in, I needed clothes, you clothed me, I was sick you and you looked after me, I was in prison and you visited me." The people He is speaking to are perplexed and respond 'When did we do these things for you?' to which Jesus responds in verse 40 "I tell you the truth, whatever you did for one of the least of these brothers of mine, you did for me." He goes on in verse 41 to rebuke the others who have not done such things for their fellow man. "Depart from me you who are cursed, into the eternal fire prepared for the devil and his angels." This account is one of many in God's Word where He shows us what is required of His children, to be called His child and share in His inheritance. The problem that I see is most people don't take the time to read God's words. I find this utterly baffling, the things people do take time to read- from romance novels to a biography of a fallen football legend- yet when it comes to the written words from the Creator of the universe we can't find time. In America we are totally without excuse. The bible is everywhere and easily accessible- even in most people's hands everyday on their phones. It is even available on audio for those who do not read. It really is a shame that most do not seek to know the Supreme Ruler in an intimate, personal way when it not only is so readily available, but also sought after by our King as well. Each relationship with God is personal, God knows every man's heart, we cannot look into another's heart. For this reason, it really is impossible for us to know for sure where ones soul goes when they pass. We do however need to take responsibility for our own relationship with God. We all will be judged. I want to hear "Well done, good and faithful servant!" don't you?

Mary's family and friends were now standing up to speak. Minerva and her husband, Freeman, tell of Mary's influence in their lives. Mary had come out of the Amish community over ten years before. Minerva had grown up Mennonite. Mennonite and Amish have very similar cultures, so that was something her and Minerva had in common. Minerva described herself as a 'broken woman' when she met Mary. She went on to describe how Mary spent many, many hours counseling and mentoring her thru her pain. I related to that hurt and brokenness. I knew how difficult it is to overcome such obstacles. My admiration for Mary grew as I listened to the impact she had on both Minerva and Freeman. Mary had served as a parental figure for Minerva and carefully scrutinized her blossoming romance with Freeman as he courted her. Freeman spoke of the strong connection he had made in a relatively short period of time. Mary seemed to have a special ability for intimate connections. The counseling that Mary had consistently given to this couple would be deeply missed. I prayed in that moment that God would somehow replace the irreplaceable.

There was another lady who had been referred to as 'adopted family'. Her name was Erma. My impression of her was one of softness. She kept a demure smile on her face and spoke quietly. I saw the hurt as she read a poem in Mary's honor. Minerva, Erma, and Mary had a unique bond. They not only had joining property lines for many years but also each shared ties to the beloved Amish/Mennonite lifestyle they left behind and the new, often stressful world they had entered. This bond transcended normal friendships. They were family. Minerva and Erma had "adopted" Mary as their surrogate mom, and she loved them as daughters. I felt the deep love as I listened to her trembling voice reading words in tribute to a treasured kindred spirit.

The next group of people to speak were not as composed as their predecessors. They were younger, appearing to be in their early twenties. Within this group was a young lady who reminded me so much of my own daughter, Shelby. Her emotions left her practically speechless as she tried to gain composure to get thru the words of homage she had committed to Mary. She referred to her as 'mom' as she continued. I cannot quote her, but her words left a huge impact on me nonetheless. She told of how her biological mother had died at a young age and Mary had taken her in. as she was speaking, Robin leaned into me and whispered:

"I forgot to tell you this! When Mary was Amish she served as a sort of 'foster parent'. If there was a child in need Mary would take care of them- in a sense she had dozens of kids! There were so many children she helped and she loved little ones, her nieces and nephews were so important to her!"

These words hit me hard. The intensity of empathy I felt was causing what had been intermittent tears to become a steady flow once again. I pictured my daughter forced to stand in front of mourners after losing me. I understood the anguish this poor young lady was suffering as she recounted calling Mary's phone just to hear her voice once more. Another loved one missing Mary would talk about formulating a text to send before the realization of her unexpected departure hit them.

Mary didn't have biological children, but she had children! Many children, many who long to hear her voice and feel her hugs. Many who looked to her for guidance and wisdom. Young people who are having trouble holding it together now that she's gone on.

"I don't know what I'm going to do without her. She was always there for me. I know she's in heaven and I'm not sad for her, but I am sad for me, right now. I will really miss her," a young lady expressed. She could barely get those words out through her tears. Her heart was breaking, and mine ached for her.

My mind was swirling with regret and uncertainty of the decision that brought me here. I truly did not wish for my presence to bring more pain to any one of the people here. I felt the despair and grief emanating from this girl as she spoke, and she seemed to look right at me. Surrounded by her cousins who all shared a deep attachment for the amazing woman no longer in their lives, she wept. The group of young people that stood in front of me now could not possibly want me to a part of this service. I again felt the urgency to escape. I thought about how to exit the building without bringing more attention to myself than there already was, but I couldn't think of any possible way. Being seated in the front of the room made an indiscreet departure not achievable. I would have to stay.

'It can't be much longer, the service has to be about over', I thought 'we will leave as soon as we can.'

Another song was sung. It was a German hymn, commonly sung in both Amish and Mennonite churches. I later learned the title translated is 'God loves me dearly'. I could not sing along, I did not know German, so it allowed me to just listen. The sound was beautiful; a church filled with hundreds of people all singing this hymn to a God who was Father to us all.

# CHAPTER 9

# MARY WAS READY

The next speaker for Mary's commemoration was Robin's husband, the former pastor of this church. What he said totally took me by surprise.

"I want everyone to know that Mary planned this entire funeral-down to the letter. She picked the songs that we have sung, the scripture that was read. She picked every person that was to speak- every part of this service was Mary's desire. She came to me last December with a request. She said she wanted my help to plan her funeral. I kinda laughed at her, telling her we didn't need to do that right now. What's the urgency? You're not sick or anything. She was persistent and here we are! We sat for hours going over details. I agreed to speak, thinking this will never happen, well maybe years down the road, but never thinking it would be this soon. But Mary knew. She at least suspected. Mary was not afraid of death, she welcomed it! She longed for the day when she would go to live with her God. She spoke of death with joy, not sorrow and wished for this memorial service to be a celebration. We are to rejoice that Mary has no more pain; she is in a grand place surrounded by angels in glory. When we think of Mary my prayer is we are happy for her."

She planned her funeral? She thought about dying to the point that she convinced her minister to take the time during the Christmas season- a super busy time of year for all preachers- to plan a funeral? God must have prepared her. I was reminded of scripture where both Peter and Paul on separate occasions, had premonitions of their own death. In 2nd Peter, Peter said God had revealed his death to him. I had read in a couple passages, one in Acts, the other in 2nd Timothy, where Paul had warned his readers that his time was soon approaching. When studying these accounts, I had often been in awe of God's desire to prepare His children for what may otherwise be a difficult subject to face- our own immortality. I, myself, have many times longed for the next chapter of this life to unfold. Death does not worry me, so I related all too well with Mary being joyful as she thought about her impending demise. I recalled once when I was with a dear friend who had not yet given her life over to Jesus and the song "I Can Only Imagine" came on over a store intercom. As I enthusiastically sang the words, picturing a day when I would come face to face with Jesus, my Lord, she abruptly stopped me.

"Do you always have to be so morbid? I've never seen anyone so fascinated with death before!"

I replied with a huge smile,

"It's not death, it's life! Don't you get it? This life isn't what it's about to me, not at all. This is just a practice run, a training ground of sorts. I am waiting for the real thing! Life is living with God; it's being face to face with Jesus and singing with the angels!"

She had heard me talk of death more than once in a way she couldn't understand. She had heard it before and would again; my convictions on that subject have only deepened thru the years.

I can't begin to explain how extremely comforting the information that he was sharing was to me. I was not shocked as some might have been, quite the opposite. It was more confirmation that Mary's relationship with God went deep. My hope was stronger than ever that we would someday meet and share our passion for Him. The idea that she had been prepared for this somehow was almost overwhelming. I had thought of death often, with eagerness, but hadn't thought to plan a funeral. That seemed to be taking it to a whole other level. And in December! We were now in October, so it had been within a year's time. I was in awe at the amazing grace of God. The immense love He has for His children that He prepares us in such a way as this. This part of the ceremony would stay with me for months to come, to remind me we are never truly alone when we belong to Him!

Robin again leaned in close and whispered,

"Mary was so ready to go! We all thought planning her funeral was unnecessary, but she was never more serious! She talked about how much she wanted to leave this earth many times to many people."

Her husband went on to tell wonderful things about Mary, most I had heard from Robin earlier. It occurred to me as he spoke that the people who were speaking had not volunteered. Mary had solicited each one of them. That explained why some of them had such a difficult time speaking to the crowd before them. Some of them had mentioned the irony of Mary's death because she had either talked to them by phone or in person about her passing. She had not wanted anyone to be caught off guard. Mary also wanted everyone to know that she was prepared and not to mourn for her. Different ones spoke of how they dismissed it at the time, but when they heard the news her words had come back to them. Mary's vision into the fate that was before her had given me a real peace. As I processed this information, I started to allow myself to attempt a sense of acceptance. Was it possible that God had a plan all along? Was this something bigger than me? Was this bigger than my limited understanding? Could it be that I didn't interfere with Divine providence, after all? But, as quickly as the thoughts entered, I chased them away. It wasn't that I didn't want to believe this, it's just years of conditioning had left me with an innate ability to turn everything bad that happened in my life into my fault. I would almost look for ways to blame myself. Taking responsibility for events like these was like a safety mechanism for me. It gave me a sense of control when things around me were so very out of control. Of course, I wasn't aware of what I was doing. It's only in retrospect that I can attempt to understand my thought process at the time. There's also the very real, although perhaps less understood, spirit world at play, as well. I know Satan is real- very real. I know that I was under attack and had been since the accident took place.

I had been studying the book of Job all week, trying to prepare some kind of lesson for the high school class that I was committed to teach on Sunday. Generally speaking my lesson planning went pretty smoothly, but not this week. I had read and reread the first couple chapters, trying to figure out how to relay the lesson that God had portrayed in this book to my students. But I was struggling. I wanted to let them know that God was in control of my situation as well. I was concerned that with circumstances being so grim, it would be difficult for them to believe that. The way I had been dealing with it, or really not dealing with it, made it feel hypocritical to teach this lesson. I knew God's truth, but was having immense difficulty importing it into my daily life. As I read through the first couple chapters, there were several things that really jumped out at me. First, was the awareness that Satan- a fallen angel- and all the angels have to check in with God periodically:

Job chapter 1: verse 6-7 reads:

"One day the angels came to present themselves before the Lord, and Satan also came with them. The Lord said to Satan, 'Where have you come from?' Satan answered the Lord, 'From roaming through the earth and going back and forth in it.'

And then again in chapter 2: verse 1-2, it says:

"On another day the angels came to present themselves before the Lord, and Satan also came with them to present himself before Him. And the Lord said to Satan, 'Where have you come from?' Satan answered the Lord, 'From roaming through the earth and going back and forth in it.'

Sometimes I think that because evil is not from God and we see so much evil that somehow we believe Satan is in control. But he's not! God is in control- all the time! Satan answers to God- God never answers to him. The ways of God are beyond our understanding. Yes, believe it or not, the creator of the world and everything in it does things that His creation does not always understand! Why does He allow evil? His creation was and is created with free will. Even the angels have free will. Satan and his demons (once angels, too) chose evil. There are some people who enjoy evil as well. A large part of faith is believing- even though we don't have all the answers. God gives us what we need to believe, the rest is on us. As I related this to my and Mary's recent events, I wondered how could God be involved in this at all? My personal connection and pain made this truth too hard to accept and apply at the time.

The second thing that stuck out to me is that God is actually the one who pointed Job out to Satan to be tested.

Job chapter 1: verse 8-12 reads:

"Then the Lord said to Satan, 'Have you considered my servant Job? There is no one on earth like him; he is blameless and upright, a man who fears God and shuns evil.'

'Does Job fear God for nothing?' Satan replied. 'Have you not put a hedge around him and his household and everything he has? You have blessed the work of his hands so that his flocks and herds are spread throughout the land. But stretch out your hand and strike everything he has and he will surely curse you to your face.'

The Lord said to Satan, 'Very well then, everything he has is in your hands, but on the man himself do not lay a finger.'"

God knows all and knew Satan would ask to put Job through the ringer. God also knew that Job was ready for this test. In a sense God not only allowed, but ordained what was to happen to Job. Why? I don't know- I'm on a need to know basis with God, so I figure it must not be essential that I know why. I can speculate that the test was to prove to Job how great his faith truly was. I could also guess that many people in Jobs life were affected by these events in ways that drew them closer to God. We know what a major impact the book of Job has had on His children for hundreds of years, especially ones going thru trials. We are not intended to know all the "whys"- we are, however instructed to have faith even when things might not make sense to us. I think of it like this- My grandson Delbert is only two. There are certain things I take the time to explain to him. For instance, don't run into the street because cars are really dangerous and they will hurt you. Does he understand?

He does on some level, but not to the extent that his five-year-old sister does. There are other things he doesn't really understand at all, like why he can't start my tractor and drive it around the yard in the same way he drives his child size four-wheeler. Do I take the time to completely explain everything to him until he totally gets it? That would be futile, at least while he remains two years old and has a two-year-old's perspective. As humans, we are like babes compared to God. His ways are so much bigger than we can even conceive. He knows explaining everything to us right now would be futile, especially while we have only our physical world to learn from. Someday, when we experience the spiritual realm, more things will become clear. Do I believe we will have it all figured out once in heaven? No way! But, I'm sure there will be things that make sense then that simply could not make sense to us now. So, what is the most important thing for us to know? I believe it's the truth that God is in control- not Satan- of everything, all the time. I knew this truth then, as well, but was not allowing it to wrap itself around me and bring me the peace that it's meant to bring.

The third thing that hit me- what I saw next, is God had to give his ok. That is obvious not only in the scripture we just read, but also in the following verses:

Job chapter 2: verse 3-6:

"Then the Lord said to Satan, 'Have you considered my servant Job? There is no one on earth like him; he is blameless and upright, a man who fears God and shuns evil. And he still maintains his integrity though you incited me against him to ruin him without reason.'

'Skin for skin!' Satan replied. 'A man will give all he has for his own life. But stretch out your hand and strike his flesh and bones, and he will surely curse you to your face!'

The Lord said to Satan, 'Very well then, he is in your hands, but you must spare his life.'"

At first Satan was not permitted to harm Job in any way, later God gave His consent. Why? Again, I don't know, but I trust God. I trust His ways are always right. There are several truths to hold onto when trying to wrap our minds around the story of Job and others like it. God created us. He knows us better than we know ourselves. He loves us more than we can fathom. God is always good. There are things we don't understand, but nothing that He doesn't know. We may identify an event as a catastrophe that God knows is a blessing. So our job is not to figure out all the answers to all the mystifying questions. Not at all! Our job is to obey when we don't understand why, to love when it seems undeserved and even impossible, and to trust Him in all things.

So as I struggled with the guilt and despair, I would not allow the truths of God to override the lies of Satan. I had read Job, attempted to come up with a lesson from it to no avail. But on this day, in this place, God's truth was all around me. God's truth was in this church. It was in these people. Mary had spoken it to those around her. God was revealing it to me in so many ways, and though I was refusing to accept it, His plan would not be thwarted. Satan would not win because ultimately, thru His people God would show me - God is in control!

The memorial proceedings were wrapping up. The final speaker was a pastor that had came all the way from Canada. He spoke of Mary in a way that made it apparent they had been very close for quite a while. Mary was very well loved and admired, I was feeling blessed to be a part of this remembrance. I felt God had led me here to get to know this wonderful person. I believed He wanted me to know she was His child, like I am. We are sisters. Though it had been difficult at times, I was really glad I had come.

# CHAPTER 10

# DON'T LOSE IT NOW

The usher had gone over to the section of the church to our right and signaled for their dismissal. That section appeared to me to consist of entirely Amish or Mennonite members. They began filing out, walking to the front of the room where Mary's body lies in the casket. The men and women walked past the coffin, somberly, most of them stopping briefly to pay respects and then walking back through the church to the rear of the sanctuary. As that side emptied out, the usher moved to our section- the center of the room. He made a gesture with his hand motioning to come forward. Robin rose to her feet, so my husband and I followed. The white bearded Amish usher, in an extremely harsh tone said,

"No! Not You! You over there!"

He had his hand held up like a crossing guard stopping oncoming traffic. He was looking right at me, as he pointed to the left front corner of the room. I felt like a child being sent to the corner after some egregious offense. Then as gruffly as he shouted at me, he softly waved Robin forward. It was the same elderly gentleman who did not want me sitting with the family. Now it seemed, he did not want me viewing Mary with them either. He took me by surprise and in my fragile state, I was beginning to lose composure. I started to feel my emotions taking over my body. The accusatory voices were resurfacing in my mind. I was certain that this man, whatever his connection to Mary, did not want her killer to be part of her wake. Robin went forward and joined her husband, the other pastors, Minerva and her husband, and Erma. They were behind the coffin prepared to receive other family and friends as they said their good byes to Mary. Delbert and I slunk over to the left side of the room. I can't remember ever feeling so alone. I was humiliated and embarrassed, but more than that. My fears were coming to volition. I had invaded an intimate family gathering and made it about me. I had exasperated an already distressing situation. My presence had affected at least one person in a negative way. If there was one, there were more than likely many. I was looking for the exit. There was just no way out! The aisle had filled in with departing family; I could not get out without further disruption to them. I needed to just wait it out.

'This will be over soon, just sit here and let them grieve! Then get out of here as soon as you can! Look what you've done!'

Thoughts started to flood my mind. Voices were screaming at me inside,

'You really did it now! You are so selfish! How dare you hurt these people on top of everything else you have done to them!'

The center pews were now clearing out and making their way to the front of the church to view Mary. This time the bereaved were not walking past the casket, they were gathering in groups of ten, maybe twenty people. Some of them I recognized as ones who spoke about Mary in the service. But the subdued, solemn atmosphere was rapidly changing to one of wailing and weeping. I watched the young loved ones fall onto Mary's body, holding onto her, not wanting to let her go. They were sobbing loudly, uncontrollably. Many were holding each other as they wept and mourned their tremendous loss.

I could hear them cry out to each other, to Mary, to God:

"What am I going to do without her? How can I go on?"

"I miss her so much already, I don't think I can do this!"

Their voices bombarded my head, they joined the already condemning ones echoing throughout.

They were becoming so loud. It felt as though there were people in the room screaming.

'You killed her! You!! Look what you took from this world! Look, look! Look at the pain you caused!'

I felt myself slipping away. I was becoming less and less aware of my conduct and was reverting back to a child-like shell. The lack of food and sleep, coupled with the horrendous burden of blame that I had put on myself was causing me to shut out the world around me. What happens at this point, my husband described to me later. I was so out of touch with reality that I became oblivious of my own behavior. Delbert would later explain to me that I was rocking back and forth and moaning or humming- he wasn't real sure which. I was sobbing uncontrollably. He attempted to reach out and touch me but I pulled away and stared at the group of people mourning at Mary's side. What I remember is looking at those beautiful people, who had suddenly lost someone they deeply loved, falling apart.

'They shouldn't have had to go through this. They shouldn't have to feel such intense pain- that's on me. I caused their anguish and now I'm here causing more!'

But mere moments into this anguish, I felt someone sit beside me. It was the same distinguished elder who had sent me to this side of the room. He was close and put his hand on me. He ever so gently, ever so kindly said these words:

"I'm very sorry. I didn't realize who you were. If I had, I wouldn't have sent you over here. You are very welcome here."

As he was comforting me, still weeping. I answered him,

"No, it's me who's sorry. I shouldn't have come. I've hurt so many people and now I'm hurting you all so much more. I am truly sorry!"

He soothingly replied,

"No, no. We want you here, Please, please stay!" and he simply turned and walked back to his duties as usher.

As I reflect on my encounter with this previously stoic figure, who had now become more of a reassuring grand father, I have to wonder what reality actually was. Could it be that Satan was messing with me? Was it possible my perception of this man was harsher than the actual reality? I now believe it's not merely possible, but most likely probable. I have come to learn through the years just how distorted our personal views can become, especially when under stress. Our individual predisposed self-evaluations can blur the lines between our mind's eye and actual reality. The impressions we have at any given time in any circumstance are greatly influenced by many other factors. Our perceptions are clouded by past experiences, our own opinions of ourselves and how others view us, and that's not to diminish the power of Satan to distort our judgment in order to further his own means. I'm sure in many scenarios other factors are also present. So I have come to the conclusion that my judgments should not always be trusted. I suppose that's why God instructs us not to pass judgment on those around us. We are simply not capable of accurately performing that duty while in this world subjected to so many variables.

His calming reassurance moved me to a more lucid awareness. My surroundings were coming back into view. The all-consuming grief and guilt that had taken over my body had started to dissipate enough to allow some sense and reason to peak through. As soon as he turned to go away, others came to me. They came one by one but at a steady pace. These were ladies there to remember Mary, yet they were coming over to care for me. I had felt segregated and ostracized just a few minutes earlier. How wrong I had been! It may have been culturally unacceptable to sit with me- I don't know, but if it was those barriers were now unimportant. Each one would sit beside me, put her arm around me and as I sobbed and muttered 'I'm sorry, I'm so, so sorry!' she would answer in a kind soothing voice:

"No, no. There's no need to be sorry. We all are so glad you came- please stay!"

She would stand up and walk away, only to allow room for the next God-sent matron waiting her turn to comfort and lavish love upon me.

"Mary is home now! It's okay, don't be sad for Mary! I'm just so glad you're here! Please stay!"

To each one as they held me I would express my remorse:

"I'm so sorry, so very, very sorry!"

And every one of them responded the same as the one who came before:

"Don't be sorry. We are so happy you came. We want you to stay- will you please stay?"

"Mary wouldn't want you to mourn. She is with God! Please stay!"

There must have been twenty to thirty ladies who made their way over to me to reach out and bring some peace. The common thing that they all repeated was for me to stay. I suppose my desire to leave was obvious. But I would later learn, their desire to know me was as intense as mine was to know them. The women stayed with me until the time came for the section we were sitting in to depart. My husband and I waited until the entire section had time to go up and pay their respects. Unbeknownst to me, Minerva and the others who had been gathered around Mary had exited earlier. Delbert and I stood up to leave; we turned to each other and mutually agreed it was time for us to go. Even with the acceptance that had just been poured out. I still felt I had most likely stepped out of place by coming. I had made a commitment to myself to not lose composure and become the center of attention. I now realized how foolish it was to believe I could achieve that. I had become a spectacle. I had taken those who came to concentrate on Mary's life into the disturbing aberration of mine. This service was about Mary and her life. She deserved to be remembered without my baggage. I would no longer take that away from them. We made our way out of the sanctuary and into the foyer, hoping to depart without encumbrance. As we neared the foyer, I saw Minerva working her way through the crowd to get to us. She was doing her best to catch us before we left.

"Are you leaving? We really want you to go with us to the gravesite? Will you come with us? "

I looked at my husband and answered,

"No, we are leaving now."

This was the first time I had expressed my opinion about anything that day. I was there for others, so I did what I was told. But at this point I knew myself well enough to fear my ability to hold it together. I was barely holding it together as I stood there facing her then. To lose control emotionally again would make my presence here deplorable. Minerva appealed once more,

"Well, okay, if you have to leave, but the family still wants to meet you. They want to hear anything you can tell them about the accident. They want to know about Mary's last minutes, whatever you could tell them."

Inside my stomach was doing flips, my head was throbbing. The very last thing I wanted to do was stay at this point, but what she said resonated with me. When my brother died, I wanted to know what he went through at the end so badly. I wondered if he suffered. I had a chance to ease that burden for Mary's family. I knew she did not suffer. I saw her immediately and she appeared at peace, sleeping. I know now she was in a coma. I could share this with them and perhaps save someone the turmoil that I went thru imagining the worst every time I thought of my brother's passing.

"Okay, we'll stay. That's why we're here, anything I can do to help. I really don't remember much about the actual accident, but I can tell you what I've been told by the witness accounts and police officers."

"Great! We're splitting into two groups; there aren't enough cars for everyone to go, so half of the family is staying here. The cafeteria is downstairs. Go have something to eat while you're waiting."

In my mind, I was thinking:

'Eat? I couldn't eat, but…

Okay, I can meet with a few of the family members, give them the limited information that I have and get out of here- before I have another break-down.'

I believe at this point I could've left and had some healing. I had forgiveness from some and a sense of acceptance. After all, those who had made their way to me in that sanctuary were Mary's family, I was sure of it. They had walked over from the section reserved for immediate family. They had reached out to me to make sure I knew they cared for me. They must have forgiven me. I could've left now and started the healing process. I had hope that Mary was with God. I also had a clear image of Mary in my mind of a living, vibrant person, instead of the nearly lifeless image that had haunted me in the week previous. I could've left and moved on- but God wasn't done yet!

I saw a ladies room in the foyer directly to my left.

'I'll go in there and just wait it out.'

I slipped through the family who had gathered in the hallway, perhaps reminiscing about past experiences with their beloved Mary, to seclude myself in the restroom. This facility was set up with a sitting/ powder room behind the first door and the lavatory area behind a second door. As I entered the first door I passed a couple ladies conversing quietly. I smiled demurely and quickly scrambled through the next door to a vacant stall. Once in that area my body began to tremble. I started shaking uncontrollably. Feeling my knees about to give way, I grabbed onto the stall door to keep from crumpling to the floor. Every emotion that was inside me was rapidly making its way to the surface. The hours of stifling feelings and pushing them down inside were now catching up with me in full force. If I had been controlling them on any level before I most certainly was not now. I was alone and my whole body knew it. The part of my brain that forced composure was not functioning at this point and I was losing it completely. My tears became weeping, weeping became sobbing, sobbing turned into bawling.

I didn't want to do this! I had to pull it together!

'There wasn't much farther to go, we could leave soon, just get it together for a little longer!'

I heard my voice, speaking out loud,

"Get it together! You have to get it together! Stop doing this! Stop!"

I started to beg God for help. "Please God! Please! I can't do this! I'm not strong enough to do this! Give me the strength to give Mary's family what they need. I can't do this by myself! I need you! I need your strength! Please, please give me strength!

I stood splashing my face with cold water to try to get a grip on my upheaval of emotion when I looked up into the mirror and saw the broken, battered face staring back at me. As I looked into those hurting eyes, I felt no compassion. All I felt was contempt, contempt for a person who had no resilience, no ability to take on life's challenges.

"Oh, God I'm not strong, I just can't do this, I'm sorry I just can't!"

My voice must have carried through the door. I had no idea that there were a group of women congregating outside the door in the waiting area between the lavatory and foyer. I had no idea they were there, but they knew where I was. They were well aware of my presence.

The creak of the door alerted me to women coming into the room. They were apparently Mary's family, Amish ladies who most likely knew her all of her life. They were gathering around me, wrapping their arms around me-eight maybe ten of them encompassed me with incredible love and support. The bathroom had filled with caring ambassadors of God's love. They had crowded in until no one else could possibly squeeze in. The lady closest to me, holding me as if I were her dearest child, spoke into my ear.

"You are strong! I know you're strong! Do you know how I know you're so strong?"

She asked this question with such passion. The question was obviously rhetorical, she was setting me up for the most profound statement of my entire life. She pulled away from my ear and stood inches away from my face, looking me directly in the eyes with a look that pierced my very soul she continued,

"I know you're strong because God chose you! He chose you to bring Mary home! He needed someone strong to carry out His divine plan and He chose you!"

Wow! Those words stunned me! I had spent the last several days believing I had done something so wrong, so evil that it had thrown God's plans off-kilter. I knew God had a plan- He always does. Things that happen are not random in God's world, He has purpose. But somehow Satan had used my pride and arrogance to convince me that I, without malicious intent, had the power to throw God off His game and cause His plan to go awry. In her simple words, said to me with such fervor and certainty, I felt the truth. I heard her words and the conviction by which she said them permeated through me to my very core.

I was crying heavily and thru the tears, adamantly proclaimed,

"I'm sorry, so, so sorry! I don't feel strong. But I need you to know how very sorry I am!"

The ladies who surrounded me, now with arms around me and hands on me, were all loving me thru words of counsel and encouragement. I was truly in the midst of saints. God had brought me to this place of healing. He had a plan and this was part of it. This much love can only be the grace of God Himself! One of the ladies worked her way closer to me to be sure I would hear her words of affirmation,

"We all are so glad you came, we have longed to meet you. Please don't feel bad for Mary. She is with God now. It was only an accident."

I observed her kind face and sweet smile amid her look of concern for my well-being and I responded,

"I am sorry I took her from you. It's my fault that she's not here anymore."

"No, no don't look at it like that. We don't. We know it was Mary's time. We don't understand God's ways or why He picked you to help fulfill that plan. But you have been blessed. You had the honor of being part of that divine plan."

Blessed? Honor? Chosen? They were telling me that I was part of something bigger than me, bigger than all of us. They were ready to accept Mary's death as an ordained event because they understood God's absolute power in all things. They understood that we were created for Him not He for us. As Christians we serve Him, He does not answer to us any more than He answers to Satan. When He decides it's time for one of His creation to go home to Him, that's His decision to make. Sometimes

He chooses us to be part of that sovereign design. I was again reminded of what Job said after his children and servants were taken from this earth: "Naked I came from my mother's womb, and naked I will depart. The Lord gave and the Lord has taken away. May the name of the Lord be praised." {Job chapter 1:21}

They consoled and reassured me for several minutes, and as I gained composure I thanked them all and we dispersed into the hallway. We went our separate ways. I met up with Delbert.

There were many people in the hall when I walked out of the ladies room. They had given me the courage to venture out those doors, but now once on the outside I felt that confidence waning. I wanted to tell Delbert what I had just experienced, but as I looked around me and saw all those who had congregated there, I thought I will tell him later in a more intimate setting. Those who had stayed behind foregoing the graveside commencement were many. I realized standing there how uncomfortable it was for me still. The demons I faced were a strong force. Overpowering the love and kindness was this deep-seated predisposed, completely irreconcilable and reprehensible feeling of unacceptance. How could I believe Mary's family had accepted me when I couldn't accept myself? This personal truth I carried was now making itself known again through my entire being. I walked thru the people with my eyes pointed down to the floor, shamefully slumped in posture. When I would glimpse at someone who I believed to be a member of that Methodist church, I would allow some eye contact and perhaps a fleeting 'Hello', but for Mary's family I had only regret for the pain I caused. As I reflect on these moments, mere minutes from when I had felt such tremendous relief and healing, I can't help but marvel at the power our negative thoughts can have on us. Our perception becomes our reality. We are who we believe we are if we allow them to blind us from God's truth.

# CHAPTER 11

# A GLIMPSE INTO HEAVEN

Delbert and I decided to go downstairs to the cafeteria. He was hungry and I didn't want to be left alone anymore. I knew how weak and vulnerable to a break down I actually was. He went to the line and stood with the others waiting to be served. I went into the large open room filled with tables and chairs meant for feast and fellowship. I made my way to the back of the room, to a table unoccupied except for a lone woman who had welcomed me a few minutes earlier. The other side of the room had tables filled with Mary's relatives, people she no doubt grew up with. The room was big enough and the distance between the two groups of people far enough that I thought I could remove myself from them and perhaps not disturb the fellowship they were enjoying. The woman I decided to sit down from, looked up and smiled at me. She introduced herself and I replied,

"I'm the one who hit Mary." As I heard my own words I thought that is who I am now- my identity. My name doesn't matter. I am the one who took Mary's life. My significance, especially in this place, is as the driver of the truck who hit Mary's van. I didn't tell her my name.

"Oh, I'm so sorry. I know this must be very difficult for you."

I just nodded and stared down at the table. I knew in my head my actions were not appropriate.

'You're being rude. Say something to her! Look at her!'

I forced myself to look up and managed a sort of smile as we made small talk asking each other about family and home life. I felt she was being polite and not really interested but welcomed any conversation that took my mind away from the judgmental undertones racing thru my mind.

Delbert had sat beside us and joined in the discussion. It was a relief to have him there to carry on the channel of communication expected in these venues. I am normally very social and out spoken, but now an awkward, regressed persona had overtaken me. The familiarity of this closed up person from my past was all too real. She frightened me. I had not wished to view the world thru her eyes ever again, but here she was once more.

In very short order, a sweet Mennonite couple came and welcomed us. We exchanged pleasantries and they went on to tell us an intimately personal tragedy from their not so distant past. Their son had been driving and there had been a horrible accident, killing his girlfriend. They had felt the pain and anguish associated with such a hard life event. The mother went on to describe the distress she felt as she watched her son go through what I was experiencing now.

"That's horrible I'm so sorry for you all. It would be so much harder to watch my child suffer through such heartbreak." My response was completely sincere and heartfelt. It is so much more difficult for a parent when their child aches. We would rather take on their pain than have them feel it. I hurt deeply for her.

She expressed how God had gotten them through it and her absolute gratefulness for the forgiveness from the other family. She understood. She had gone through this and worse and was on the other side now. Her words of encouragement left me with a measure of hope. She and her husband sat and talked to us for some time before returning to their table.

It was only seconds before more wonderful members of Mary's family came over to greet us as we sat pondering the reception from the people there. Another lovely lady holds out her arms to embrace me as her more reserved husband holds his hand out to Delbert. She hugs tight just as the others before her had. Tears inadvertently ran down my cheeks every time I felt the warmth of these gestures of love and friendship.

"I'm sorry, so sorry."

To every person who stepped out to welcome me, I was given the opportunity to express my sorrow and remorse. This had amazing therapeutic power for me. It unburdened my spirit to be able to say those words and see their reactions of acceptance.

"There is no need to apologize and no need for forgiveness, because you have done nothing to be forgiven for. God always has a plan. You need to know that you were only a vessel in His divine plan. We are just so glad you are here. We have been praying for you."

I began to notice a common thread that ran thru this body of believers. They were happy. It went beyond a superficial happiness that most of us enjoy. This was a joy-filled existence. It was a life of peace in all circumstances. The true joy of the Lord that I had so often read about in scripture was radiating from them. I knew Mary had felt that joy too. It's the kind of thing that can't be rationally explained. In a time when the tragic circumstances around them should have rendered them heart broken in the eyes of the world, these children of God knew a different realism. They knew the joy that comes from knowing God has dominion over all; the joy that comes from a faith that guarantees His ways are always perfect.

As soon as that couple walked away another came. The words they said to me were all so similar in nature,

"We have been praying for you."

"We're so glad you came."

"Mary is home with God, God had a plan and took her home."

"I can't be sad for Mary. She has finished the race and won her prize."

"You were chosen."

This statement that had meant so much to me the first time I heard it would be echoed throughout the day.

Another couple sat beside us at our table and shared their story of misfortune. There had been a buggy accident that had taken another precious life. The driver of that buggy was not harmed but, like me, suffered the responsibility and guilt associated with a lost life. The story had so many similarities to mine. They knew all too well what major role forgiveness could play in the mending of ones soul after such devastation.

Not only is forgiveness essential for the guilt-ridden party, but the victim as well. When we refuse to forgive we put ourselves in a dark place. We remove ourselves from God's grace and the hate and negativity permeate every aspect of our lives. I know it's difficult, often, to achieve such a forgiving spirit. That's when we need to rely on God's Holy Spirit to guide us. This takes effort on our parts, we must actively seek that healing day after day, even minute by minute until it's achieved. I know this fact as well as anyone. Part of the mistreatment I suffered as a child was molestation and sexual abuse. Of everything I encountered in my life this was the most difficult to get past. Many times in my journey toward forgiveness I looked to the story of Joseph (found in Genesis chapters 37-50). Joseph had been betrayed by those who should have protected him, his older brothers. So betrayed that forgiveness did not come easy. He struggled for many years while God took him thru the process to the place where he could truly forgive and move on without resentment. In his case, time was an essential part of his progression toward the goal of absolution. I learned that forgiveness is often a process. It does not always happen overnight, but we need to be working toward that goal and allowing God's amazing grace to cover us as we are on that journey. The danger comes when we become so callous and resentful that we choose not to absolve those who wrong us and we don't even attempt it. Forgiveness, just like love, is a choice. It's not always an easy choice, but we have the power to choose, nonetheless.

Literally, dozens of people approached to greet me and convey their delight at my attendance.

"We are overjoyed that you came. You have been in our prayers. You have no idea how important it is for so many of us here to get to meet you. I have been so worried about how you were coping through what must be a horrible time for you."

My grief transparent as I answered,

"I am truly sorry. Thank you so much. You all have been so generous. I don't know what to say."

"How are you handling this, are you doing okay?" She asked with such sincere compassion.

"I'm so much better now." I replied, recognizing the calm that was replacing the turmoil inside my body. "The love that I have felt here is so amazing! I can't begin to tell you what it means to me!"

The words being spoken were mostly brief, lasting only a few minutes. But the impact they had on me would last a lifetime. The 100+ people in that room had all made their way to the far corner of the cafeteria where I had attempted to hide out. They came, not all at once, but in groups of two or three, some individually as not to overwhelm me. Finally one of them mustered the courage to pose the question that I later discovered they all wanted to ask.

"Can you tell us about the accident?"

"Absolutely! Well, I will try. I hit my head and I don't remember what actually caused it, but I can tell you what I've been told. I was with Mary, so I can tell you about that too."

As I went through the events of that evening with her, a crowd started to gather behind her. In my estimation around fifteen or so people had heard the request and came to hear my story. To my complete shock, I was able to go through the details completely composed. I looked at the faces before me, eager to hear anything I could tell them to bring some sense of reality to their loss, I could see how important the details were to them.

"Where did the others around Mary's van come from?"

"I'm sorry. I don't know. I think they must have been witnesses, maybe in the cars sitting in the stopped traffic ahead, I'm not sure."

"Did her airbag deploy?"

"No, but she was hit from behind so, I guess it wouldn't."

I felt some of the questions strange, inconsequential or irrelevant, but I would do my best to answer each and every one. Minerva would later explain to me that in the Amish/Mennonite culture details are very important. They regale stories with in-depth specificity. I would tell that story over a dozen times that day, until everyone who wanted to hear it had the chance. And to my utter amazement, I was able to tell it each time with complete serenity. God gave me the strength that I had asked for, the strength that I had been told was inside me. I knew then that it was inside me because I had the Spirit of God inside; all I needed to do was tap in to His power.

I was met by another lovely lady who, arms open wide, came to me with words of wisdom. She quoted one of my favorite verses in the bible. It's from the book of Isaiah chapter 55 and verse 8:

"'For my thoughts are not your thoughts, neither are your ways my ways', declares the Lord.'

"I love that verse!" I answered.

"Those words are true, we can't know all the reasons why God does what He does and the times that He chooses to do them in. But we can know that He has His reasons and they are perfect!"

"Thank you, thank you so much for that!"

She was still standing with me when a man walked past. He did not stop, he kept walking, but as he walked he said,

"And He doesn't make mistakes!"

His words were so simple, but to me so profound. I had spent all week feeling like I was a mistake. That word had infiltrated my thoughts and wreaked havoc over and over. This straightforward, uncomplicated few words coming from him, so fleeting he didn't even need to slow down to utter them, penetrated me.

The family members who had traveled to the cemetery were now returning. The once large open space of the cafeteria was now abuzz with greetings exchanged from reunions of familiar but greatly missed faces from days gone by. Funerals are bittersweet in that respect. Those attending are there to say good-bye to one they will dearly miss, but also are joining loved ones who they may not have seen for many years. I could hear happiness in the voices around. It was a pleasant sound and I couldn't help but think it was the sound Mary would have wanted at her service.

I had told the story to several groups who had gathered to hear the details and now had determined to share it with as many as I could. It had occurred to me that many might not ask; worried about the toll it might take on me to relive it. I had come to the awareness that the concern for my welfare in that room far exceeded the desire to fulfill any individual wishes. So as Mary's more immediate family connections came to introduce themselves to me and offer their friendship, I would respond by first presenting my apologies (which I came to recognize were more important to me than to them) and then quickly ask if they wanted to hear about the accident.

As the others came in, many new faces appeared, many who had ties to Mary and would have a vacancy now in their lives. I needed to get to each one of them and express my regret for the events that led to their loss. I didn't have to go to them because they all came to me, anxious to meet me and make sure I was doing okay.

"I want you to know you have not left my thoughts since this happened. I've been so concerned about you! How are you doing? Physically and emotionally? Does your head hurt much?"

I had nearly forgotten what I must have looked like to those around me. The swelling in my head had receded somewhat but was still very unsightly and incredibly bruised.

"It's okay. I mean I have headaches and my hand bothers me, but it's nothing really. The emotional stuff is really the tough part." I answered, still in awe at the worry spent on my behalf.

"I can imagine! But you shouldn't feel bad. I know God was in control. This was about Mary and how He could get her home to be with Him. You were just the instrument He used to get her there. It's you I worry about. We all know Mary is better than ever -she is with God. But you have to be okay too. His plan is not complete until you are healed both inside and out. As Mary's family we have a responsibility to see this through to the end and you are very much a part of His plan. We all have gathered to pray for you, you can't begin to imagine how much you mean to all of us."

I was speechless. Her words were so humbling, and uplifting all at the same time. We both had tears. But these were healing tears that fell from me now. I was starting to get it. Grace was beginning to get thru and mend the broken child within. I thanked her again and exchanged another hug, as I turned to greet another family member waiting to comfort the stranger in the room.

She was smiling with a sparkle in her eye. I held out my arms to hug her and whispered once more,

"I'm sorry. I want you to know that I'm sorry."

"She pulled away just far enough to make eye contact. As she looked into my eyes she stated with great resolution,

"Oh, no! No apology is needed. No forgiveness is needed! I believe with every part of my being that it was Mary's time. I understand that no one has an explanation for this accident, well I have one. I believe God put a block in your vision just long enough for you to carry out this mission for Him. Do you know Mary wanted to go in her car? Yes, Mary knew her time was near, she talked about it often. She had told people that she would like to die in her van, but she was afraid of pain. I understand that she felt no pain. God truly blessed His daughter, Mary. He gave her everything she asked for. But Mary would not want you to suffer so that she could be so blessed. Mary would want to know that you were blessed too."

Mary would want to know that I was blessed? How could this lead to blessing for me? I would soon realize that with God all things are possible. I would know why scripture says:

"And we know that for those who love God all things work together for good, for those who are called according to His purpose." (Romans 8:28, ESV)

I was greeted next by a joyful man. Distinguished? -Yes! They all were. But this man had an aura about him that made you feel good just being in his presence. He had a smile that never left his face and it was contagious. I just felt better being in his presence. He introduced himself and it took me back.

"Hi, I'm Paul, Mary's brother...."

Mary's brother? He seemed to have such a joyful spirit.

"I'm sorry, very sorry."

I said to him as I pondered his apparent joy.

"You know I talked to Mary that morning on the phone. She had spoke about her death. I believe she was ready to go. I think somehow she knew. I phoned her again around the time of the accident and she didn't answer. I thought it was odd. I tried again a few minutes later. I knew something was wrong, well I guess she knew...."

"I see you're hurting," he continued, "but please remember this- 'Grieve, but only for a little while'. It's a saying we say a lot. I want you to remember it because Mary would not have you grieve for long. God has given her to us for a time and now He has taken her back so if you choose to grieve for very long it would be a disservice to Mary and her God. We need to be happy for her. So only grieve a little while for Mary."

I held out my hand and shook his, thinking of how remarkable the people here were and how blessed a life Mary must have had. I wondered if they realize how tortured so many people in this world are without the peace of God in their lives. I am in a place where God is in the fore-ground where He should be, but seldom is. The feeling of euphoria was breathtaking.

I was standing in a room surrounded by strangers who felt like family, many of them had told me I was now a part of their family. The outpouring of genuine love and acceptance was over whelming. I had to stop a minute and catch my breath, to actually take it all in and experience the moment. The room was full of people who wanted to lavish mercy and grace on me so a moment was all I got. Another group had gathered around to hear the story told again. I had told it countless times to nearly everyone there. I volunteered to tell it again to everyone that I saw. It seemed to be so healing for them. I would mention how I prayed for Mary and as I glanced up someone would be holding their hands up in the air and saying 'Praise God! Praise God!' Some people would be impacted by one part of the events and another by something else.

"I tried to give her cpr, but my hand was so banged up that I couldn't! I knew I needed to back away and give them room to work, but I didn't want to leave her!" I recalled.

Someone cried out,

"Oh no, no! She didn't want cpr-she was ready to go. You did what Mary would have wanted you to do- prayed and loved her!"

As I told of how the van had no back seats anymore from the impact, someone responded,

"Wow! Mary hauled people around so often, you know she loved to drive for us whenever we needed anything. God made sure she didn't have passengers when He took her! Praise God!"

I spoke of the connection I felt to her and I heard the response,

"Because you are connected. You were involved in the most important part of her life- her transition from this life to the next. It's a huge privilege to have that role in her life, I'm sure she is waiting to welcome you someday!"

"God has spared you for a reason! It's amazing that you survived and had such little injury. It was Mary's time, of that I have no doubt! But I'm just as certain that you were in His divine plan as well! There is some reason that he took Mary but left you here."

While they gathered around to hear me tell all the details that I could recall, the atmosphere was not one of contempt or disapproval. It did not have the mood of gloom or sadness. Quite amazingly there was more a mood of bliss and peace. It was surreal in a sense, but I totally understood it. The hope that Mary is with God now turned the chaos and destruction at the crash site into a pathway to heaven. It was true. Having sorrow for someone who is in the arms of Jesus was not logical, and they had faith that's where she is, so who can mourn?

The crowd dispersed once more and individuals again were making their way to me to give me a hug and just tell me they were glad I was there.

I caught a glimpse of a young girl heading in my direction. It was one of the girls who spoke about Mary; someone who referred to her as 'Mom'.

I walked toward her to meet her half way. She had dried her tears from when I had first encountered her. As she approached, her countenance began to change. She was fighting back the tears as she tried to speak.

"I had to come over and welcome you here."

She said, tears streaming down her face and her voice shaky.

"I didn't want you to think I had hard feelings. It's not that, not that at all. I just miss her so very much."

As I held her, my heart broke for her.

"I understand, I really do and I am so very sorry for what you're going through."

She struggled to get her words out,

"But you must know I am glad you are here and I don't have any bad feelings. I believe it was God's plan. She tried to prepare me. She tried to prepare a lot of us. It's just too hard to be ready for something like this, at least it is for me."

"I'm sure it is. It's so sweet of you to come over. I will pray for you. I am very sorry, very sorry."

This was the hard part. When I felt the pain with those who don't know how to move on without such a vital part of their life. What do I say? There truly aren't words.

This kind-hearted soul stepped back to let another move in closer. A lovely woman with a gentle face and quiet, timid voice held onto my arms.

"How are you? I have prayed so earnestly for you! You know we are not in any way bitter. Forgiveness is a command from God; Mary would not want any bitterness! You are like family to us we need to know you are going to be okay. This was God's will."

I held her arms as well, and I tried to answer in kind,

"I still need to tell you I am sorry. But I do so appreciate your thoughtfulness."

She smiled and nodded as she walked away allowing room for another sweet soul who wanted to console and pardon me. Someone came up behind and gently whispered in my ear,

"Do you know that was Mary's sister."

Mary's sister?! I had to talk to her again! Her only sister, where did she go? I must see her again! I excused myself from the person waiting to share with me and rushed to locate her! She had only gone a few feet and I exclaimed,

"Wait!"

She stopped immediately and glanced back in my direction, I pushed through the people ignoring my sudden insolence and caught up to her. I said with exuberance,

"You're Mary's sister? Her only sister?!"

I reached out to hug her and she opened her arms as well.

"I'm so very sorry, so so very sorry! I have one sister too! I know how hard it would be to lose her!"

I had dried my tears probably an hour before. Those around me had flooded my heart with love and forgiveness so much that my sorrow had turned to joy with theirs. But they came rushing back now! I sobbed as I embraced her thinking of her extreme kindness midst what had to be tremendous sorrow. She looked at me and with the gentleness of a lamb said,

"I will miss her, of course I will miss her, but we can't be sad for Mary. So should I be sad for me? No, I will rejoice for Mary! God gave a sister and I had her for 62 years, it's time for Him to take her back. I can't be upset about that. But, yes I will miss her!" she said thru her tears.

Her selflessness gave me pause. I wondered if I could be as gracious if my sister were just taken.

The afternoon had progressed into nearly the evening hours! We had spent an entire day with these gracious people. We felt it was now time to go. Looking around it seemed I had spoken to each and every one of them! What a blessing I received! The most amazing part is that they each had received a blessing as well. I had developed friendships- no much more than that- family connections that would last a lifetime. As Delbert and I were saying our good byes, Paul came over to say his. We exchanged pleasantries and business cards, got emails and phone numbers of those who had them.

"I wish I would have heard the details of Mary's passing. I never seemed to get over to you in time while you were telling it." he casually stated, as if in passing.

"What? You didn't get to hear to it?"

"No" he said, not wishing to put me out. "But you should leave, it's okay. I'll just hear it from my sister, Barbara."

"Oh no you won't! You are Mary's brother! You are going to hear it straight from me- and if you have any questions you are going to ask me! I want all of your questions answered!"

So I went on to tell the story one last time, well one last time on that day. And a crowd gathered around once more as if there was a grandfather reading a Christmas story. There were 'Amens!' and 'Praise the Lords', raised hands and eyes closed worshipping God, but I had come to expect nothing less!

Delbert and I walked out of that church with a sense of exhilaration! What a roller coaster of emotion this day had brought! I had awakened in the morning with a feeling of hope and God had exceeded every aspiration I had had. We looked at each other with broad smiles; and each kind of shook our heads in disbelief.

What just happened?

It didn't feel real. The intensity of emotion and adrenaline that was surging through us must have been what the apostle Paul referred to as a 'mountaintop experience', when he wrote about experiencing God on such a deep, personal level. Yeah, I would say mountaintop says it about as well as anything.

As we got into our car to head back home, I said:

"Wow! That was amazing! I feel like I've just stepped out of heaven! It's so strange, but I miss them already. It's really hard to leave. Do you know what I mean?"

"I do! I totally do! That must be what heaven is like, all that love and kindness! And everyone put God first above their own personal wants. It was awesome, just awesome!"

As Delbert replied to me, I saw a look on his face that I will never forget. It was peaceful, and exhilarating all at the same time. I knew my expression must have been the same.

We sat in silence a large part of the drive. That is very unusual for us, but I understood why. Neither one of us wanted to fill the air with mundane, superficial chatter after what we just experienced. We were awestruck and we didn't want the feeling to end.

"We have to tell the Sunday school class about this, they all have been praying. Well, I guess our whole church has been praying!" Delbert said, breaking the quiet stillness. "So many people have been praying-other churches, too, you know."

He went on to mention co-workers and family, neighbors, people I barely even knew. There were people who had long sense moved away who at one time attended our church who had their churches praying. The church that I had grown up in as a child was also praying. The petitions reaching heaven must have been thunderous to God! So many faithful followers resounding concern for me- that by itself was overwhelming to think about!

"Not only all of them, but think about it! Every person we just left has been praying for us too! It's too incredible to wrap my mind around-all the people this incident has affected and brought closer to God in some way!" I marveled.

I knew what an impact praying for others could have on a person's relationship with God. Years earlier a dear lady in our church and close family friend had a recurring health issue that rendered her weak and in the hospital with seizures. Our church family's heart was breaking to see her go thru this once again and we all wanted to do something. So the idea came to pray around the clock. A schedule was set up with a sign up sheet and members would take a minimum of fifteen minutes to pray for her specifically. I decided to take several different time slots, two of which were in the middle of the night when I normally would be sleeping. I knew with her extreme seizure activity, there were many sleepless nights for her and those volunteering to sit with her, so I felt prayers were vital at those times. Through that experience I had regained a more intimate connection with God. Making time and specifically honoring and trusting Him gave me a sense of closeness deeper than I had had before. I heard from many others that the same thing was happening for them.

The power of prayer is colossal. I have seen God do things after fasting and praying that took my breath away. Here it is happening again. I knew on that drive home that I had been restored. I knew that broken, battered face that I saw in the mirror just a few hours earlier would not condemn me when I looked back at it the next time. I felt renewed. To say that I was restored to where I had been before the accident would be an inaccuracy. I was not as before, I was better than I had ever been! But that's what God does, when He gives us new life it's better than ever before! I reminisced about the things that were said, words that were used-

"Chosen", "Blessed", "Honor", "Privilege", "Instrument", Vessel", "God's plan"

I had words of affirmation going through my head, instead of words of disapproval and blame. They had become my new personal truths. I couldn't deny them because God had taken so much time and energy to give them to me. He would not let me leave without revealing His truth. And he chose 400 Amish people to deliver His message that day! I had to smile when I thought about it,

'It took 400 Amish people to get you out of the state you had put yourself in!'

As I contemplated the reality of that thought, I realized I wouldn't have listened to anyone except those who knew Mary. It had to come from people who were missing her and felt the loss, because only they could absolve my guilt. In God's supreme wisdom and grace, He knew that and He brought them to me-or in essence brought me to them. I thought to myself, how could I allow the guilt and despair back into my life now? It would be so offensive, not only to God, but to Mary's family who worked so hard to make me whole again! I set my mind- then and there!

'You will NOT feel guilt or sorrow anymore because God has proven to you that He was there when you had the accident. He may not have caused it, put up a block in your vision as some of Mary's family believed, but He was there! Of that you are certain. He prepared Mary and her family. My hope was restored. Mary was His child and He always has a plan for His children- He was there!'

I am His child too, and now I completely understood and embraced what that meant. He had a plan for me as well. I was a vital part of His plan. It was not an end, not at all. It was a beginning- for her and for me!

# CHAPTER 12

# THE POWER OF GRACE
# AND FORGIVENESS

We arrived home after the three-hour drive. We each had commented on how quickly those hours had gone by. The awareness of God's presence through out that day sent our minds whirling and had given us a 'high' that made time insignificant. Our spirits were soaring! The conversations of the day had separated Delbert and I on a few different occasions. Often, when a couple would approach, the husband would speak to Delbert, while the wife was reaching out to me, so we spent the rest of the evening sharing our individual experiences. His impressions of the people he interacted with were exactly like mine. They had used similar phrases and not one person held any animosity. The husbands had given him contact information as well, and also said they considered us family now. It was amazing! He was told multiple times that they had been praying for me. And how important it was for them to let me know of Mary's readiness, as well as the conviction that this was God's plan. We both reveled in the wonder of it all until the hour and commitments for the following day forced us to go to sleep.

I closed my eyes, and again I saw Mary. I saw Mary holding children. I saw Mary studying her bible. I saw Mary counseling other women. I saw

Mary alive and living! It was the most marvelous thing I had ever seen or felt. God had replaced my hurt with healing! He had restored my joy! I opened my eyes, smiled- thanked God, closed my eyes again and had the best night's sleep I had ever had!

On the drive home, as well as the Saturday following, I would spend some significant time calling people to let them know how amazing the day was! The reactions were all the same-tears and awe. I understood that this was not only big for me, but this was huge for everyone who heard it. Everyone has had a time in their life where we need to forgive someone, as well as a time when we need forgiveness from someone. Those times can turn into life changing experiences- good or bad. They not only alter the way we view others but can hugely affect the quality of life we live. If we have resentment in our lives it will affect every aspect of it. Many of us have an event where a lack of forgiveness is so paramount to our lives that we remember every detail of something that happened years and years before. I knew I needed to share the story with as many of my family and friends who would listen. I contacted people and set up lunch dates for the following week, telling them I needed to talk to them- I had been in an accident that had taken a life. The magnitude of that event made it difficult to refuse my invitation and my calendar was full!

Saturday morning I had worship practice at the church. I was thankful that this was my month to sing. Practicing the praise songs thru the week had really been a blessing. I left early, anticipating another opportunity to share this life-changing event. When I came through the doors, I was ready to explode as I excitedly told those there what had happened. The songs we sang had more meaning than ever. God was so real and so personal that morning. I felt so loved and cared for. I couldn't sing without tears, but these were tears of elation.

I had to teach the high school class the next morning and had struggled all week coming up with a lesson. I sat down to put something together. As I reread Job, I had a whole new perspective. All week I worried that as I taught my students, my own issues would overshadow the class and my fears and guilt would cast a shadow on the point I wanted to get thru. That point was that God is sovereign and we don't always understand His ways, but we need to trust Him. I believed it before the funeral, but if the kids had questions, personal questions about why God allowed me to hit Mary's van, I didn't know what I would say. I was afraid the uncertainty in their teacher might shake their faith. Now, as I sat and looked at the scripture before me, my eyes welled up. He had answered my prayers. I had asked Him to allow His Spirit to bring me a lesson that would not bewilder or confuse my class. Wow! Did he deliver! I decided to read the first two chapters in Job and ask some hard questions about the sovereignty of God. This is the lesson I taught that Sunday morning:

I started out by asking them if they thought God was there at my crash. Then I asked if Satan was in control for just a few minutes- long enough to hit her van. (Did God blink, or look away?)

Was it random? Was it God's plan?

My class is a young class, many still in junior high, but I'm often amazed at their maturity. They answered with "God is always in control- He never looks away!"

One student quickly and adamantly states that we aren't capable of understanding everything He does so we just need to trust Him.

From the mouths of babes! She had hit my lesson plan right on the head! It sounded so simple, but it was God's truth. I then read Psalm 91:14-15. This is a scripture that I read during the week for encouragement:

"Because he loves me," says the Lord. "I will rescue him; I will protect him for he acknowledges my name. He will call upon me and I will answer him; I will be with him in trouble, I will deliver him and honor him."

I went on to describe to the kids how broken I had become, how afraid and lost. That I really needed rescued. I told them how I sat clutching my bible having read those verses and wondering why I hadn't been rescued from that horrific accident.

'I love You, I called on You, why didn't you rescue me?' I prayed to Him.

We went on to read about Job, just the first two chapters, I told them Job's story didn't end there and mine didn't end at the crash site either. I explained that when we enter a crisis we tend to lose vision and hope, but

God doesn't end our story there. He has a plan, and we need faith, just like my student had said.

I continued by sharing the incredible funeral that I had just attended and the amazing healing that took place. I shared with them my perspective, as distorted as it was before the funeral:

'That I had killed an innocent beautiful person, by some lack of focus or judgment mistake, then that in turn encroached on God's master plan. My negligence had messed up God's perfect design'.

I then shared with them how my perspective had since been altered by God's Spirit through the grace and love of Mary's family. This was the new perspective:

'God had a plan and He either used me to fulfill that plan or in the very least allowed my unfortunate circumstances to get Mary home. Either way He wasn't finished until He made sure I was okay. Not just okay, but wonderfully blessed!'

Leaving that classroom we all had a more complete awareness of who God is. I closed with these key truths to always remember and hold onto:

God is in control- 100 % of the time

God always has purpose

God is always good

God answers prayer 100% of the time

God is Sovereign (Satan is not ever in control!)

And perhaps this is the most important truth of all:

God is God- we are not!

The week ahead was filled with meetings and lunches sharing the forgiveness and love that had been found at that Methodist church the past Friday. Every day I met at least once, and often twice to share. Every audience whether a group of twenty or an individual would be in tears. I felt the need to tell it to anyone who wanted to hear. The first two weeks directly following the funeral, my days were booked with venues to speak and lunches with old friends. The vulnerability I exposed allowed others to share their own stories with me. God was actively working and it was apparent every day.

'Mary would be so thrilled!'

I often thought to myself after leaving someone who her story had just touched.

On one occasion after I had finished recounting the story to a church bible class, a young lady came up after to speak to me. She had tears in her eyes and stammered as she tried to speak,

"Not everyone gets forgiveness."

The tears really were flowing now, as she painstakingly attempted to get her words out.

"All I can say is you are very fortunate. I hope you know that."

She quickly walked away before I had a reply. Her pain was so real and she spoke truth. Not everyone does get forgiveness. Very possibly most will not. Even when there is forgiveness, many will never experience the joy of hearing it expressed. How dreadfully sad that reality is. I wasn't really sure what to do with that. There had been a couple times before when someone would mention after I spoke, how they had been involved in an auto accident too, but the family didn't handle it the same. In both cases it had been years in the past and even though you could see some hurt, time had eased the pain on some level. They were gracious and pleased that my story had been different, so I hadn't given it that much thought. But now I was faced with the possibility that my story might cause pain to others who had different outcomes than mine. What could I do? I couldn't somehow alter the universe in a way that allowed every person to love others as Jesus taught and thus prevent pain like this poor girl and many others are feeling. God's divine plan has allowed free will and that will causes us to sin and hurt each other. Sometimes I think we don't even realize the pain our actions cause. Sometimes no action hurts others just as much. Forgiveness takes action, love takes action. When we do nothing and we know someone is hurting that we could help, we are not loving them. The usher at the funeral did not need to come over to comfort me, after all, he was a man and I was a woman of the secular world- he could have told himself it was not appropriate, let a lady do it. Or the countless others who made their way to me that day could've said to themselves that someone else is talking to her, I don't need to. But they didn't. Each and every one saw me and took action, each one set aside time to come over and let me know they loved me and held no resentment. I needed each and every one of them, and they were there. Just think how much better this world would be if each and every one of us took action when another was hurting. We seem to understand when another is in physical danger that as humans we have a responsibility to help. Most of us would not stand by and watch while a dog was attacking someone without trying to pull him to safety. Why is it that we cannot understand how much more damaging emotional pain can be in ones life? So often we have the capability to ease another's emotional burden and we simply look the other way. An excellent example of going the extra mile is Minerva. We had kept in contact after the funeral and in one of our talks she had told me her story behind my invitation to meet the family, which later became an invitation to Mary's funeral.

"You know it's incredible that we even saw your request to come at all. The family was exhausted from the viewings and we were all planning on just looking at the memorial page after things died down a little. But there was an old friend of Mary who had come from across the country to attend the funeral who was hanging out there with us. She came running over to me late that night and said 'You gotta see this!' We had been discussing how we would like to meet you, but a couple of Mary's nieces and nephews had said they didn't know if they were ready for that quite yet. When we heard that you wanted to come, we all were concerned about them, but they spoke right up and said 'yes! Have her come, it would be good for all of us.' It was crazy though because by the time we all decided and had talked it through, it had really gotten late. We figured you would never look at it, and were disappointed at that thought. We knew it would help bring healing all the way around! It's just amazing how God has worked. The timing of it all was just so awesome, I think even a few hours earlier and there would have been some who would have said 'Not yet'. It was truly a God-thing! God is so awesome!"

God is truly awesome!

## CHAPTER 13

# THE ARRAIGNMENT

About a week after the funeral, an arraignment date had been set for the following Thursday. Detective Curry had called and let me know the details for the day. He had taken great effort to arrange this with the least amount of burden to my husband and I as possible. With the courthouse around two and half hours away, he was hoping we could get the entire process over in a day. My desire was to plead guilty to the charge of vehicular homicide and work out some sort of plea arrangement. I understood that there was possible jail time with this charge, but God had shown me that He was very involved in this from the start so I felt He wasn't stopping now. Whatever He decided was fine by me. I knew God answers prayer and many were still praying. Just a couple days before the day designated for my arraignment, I was at the church following a ladies bible study. I always stop in to see the secretary of the church, Debbie, who just happens to be my one of my dearest friends. I enjoy our little moments together- just getting a hug and checking up on each other's families, seeing what's happening with kids and grand kids. When I stopped on this particular morning she arranged for the staff to all pray with me. We all stood in a circle, holding hands and each one took a turn asking for God's will to be done. I had made it clear that I didn't want anyone to pray that I didn't go to jail, because if that's where God wanted me-then that's where I wanted to be. When it came time for Debbie to pray, her prayer made me smile:

"Dear God we ask for you to be with Tracy, and I know I'm supposed to pray for your will to be done, but I really don't want her to go to jail. So I'm going to be selfish and ask that you keep her from going to jail..." (She would later tell me those in that prayer circle confessed to each other that in their private prayers they would request that I not go to jail.)

Concerned family and friends had been urging me to hire an attorney but my response was always the same:

"God's got this! I'm not worried. He has a plan and He's not finished yet. If I go to jail it will be His will. I was supposed to do a prison ministry several years ago and I put it off because of caring for a foster child at the time, so maybe this is my Jonah moment!" (In the bible we're told of a time when God commanded Jonah to go to a city that he didn't want to go to, when he refused and went the other direction, a fish swallowed him.)

I would continue:

"Joseph could have hired O.J.'s dream team and still went to prison! If God wants me there, I'm going anyway so why pay for an attorney." (The story of Joseph in the Old Testament is a favorite of mine. He went to prison on false charges, but continued to serve God- knowing He was part of a bigger plan, and he ended up being second in command to Pharoah!)

I really was not worried about jail at all. I thought it would be an excellent place to share my story- who knows how many lives might be changed!

Detective Curry had worked it out so that I could show up and turn myself in on Thursday. That was the day that the courthouse should have both the prosecutor and the public defender there, along with a judge that could render sentence once one was agreed upon. He wasn't sure if it could all be done in a day, but Thursday gave us the best shot. I had gotten ready for the possibility that I might not be coming home. I run a horse farm and had to move some horses around, get some large round bales of hay set out and make sure each had some sort of water and shelter if I wouldn't be home to let them in the barn at night or in the case of bad weather. I was prepared for whatever came next and really just wanted to be able to put this part of it behind me.

The detective asked me to get there an hour early to make sure I had time to be processed, mug shots, fingerprints, and any other official things that might need done before we went to the courthouse. He wanted us at the courthouse by nine to catch the lawyers before they were involved with other cases. Delbert and I got there almost two hours early.

Delbert had brought his bible in with him so he would have something to occupy the time and he sat down and started to read once we got inside.

"Delbert, I really need to use the restroom, can you sign me in?" I asked as he was putting his reading glasses on.

He assured me that he would, and I headed to the restroom. I splashed my face with water; most of the swelling and bruising was gone now. Just a single bruised bump that I was able to hide under my bangs remained. I took a deep breath and went back out to the lobby.

"You signed me in, right?"

"Yep, all signed in." he replied, not even looking up from his bible.

A police officer walked by us as we were sitting there. Smiling, he asked Delbert .

"Reading the good book, huh?"

Delbert responded with a smile,

"Sure am!"

The officer, still smiling went on,

"Why are you guys here, may I ask?"

Delbert told him about the accident, and his smile changed to heart felt compassion.

"Do you mind if I have my church pray for you, and of course my family and I as well?"

"Absolutely! That would be great! We really appreciate that!" Delbert responded.

"Thank you very much! We really do appreciate it! Thank you!" I chimed in.

He continued out as we continued waiting. Just a few minutes later he returned, but this time he had brought another officer with him.

"We would like to pray with you here if you would like us to. Would that be alright?" the officer asked us.

"That would be great! Yes, definitely! Thank you!"

We gathered in a circle there in the lobby of the police station, much like the church staff had done with me a couple days before. But these were strangers- we had never met before, yet here we stood hand-in-hand praying as one. Both of the officers prayed out loud in a public police station lobby. It had to be one of the most awesome moments of my life! God was letting us know that He had this. He was there with us-in that room and it was important to Him that we knew it. It wasn't just about me; Delbert was more worried than I was at this point. I had resigned myself to do whatever came next and was actually excited to see what was coming. But Delbert was afraid to lose his wife. We had heard this particular charge could carry up to a three-year jail term. He didn't want me to go away. He needed to feel God's presence as much or more than I did.

As the day went on, we would see these officers here and there. Each time it was like God was sending His angels to reassure us that He still has this under control!

Shortly after our prayer time, a young lady came in. She must have been late teens or early twenties. She was crying as she went up to the receptionist window,

"I need to finish making my statement." I could hear her, I was not eves dropping but she was only a few feet from me. The receptionist, being a few feet back from her, was out of ear shod. But must have asked her name,

"Ashley" she replied.

"I started my statement while I was in the hospital, with a policeman there. I was supposed to come back here to finish it."

The receptionist must have asked what it was about, because she replied:

"I, I was assaulted and, uh, kidnapped. She stammered as she fought back tears.

I felt so bad for her. It was obvious the trauma she had suffered, you could hear it in her voice. The lady at the window must have told her to have a seat, because she turned and found a chair.

She sat on the other side of the room from where Delbert and I were seated. I got up and went to her. She was shaking at this point and weeping more than before. I put my arms around her, remembering how comforting the arms of Mary's family members had been to me. She hugged me back and wept more profusely. As I held her, I prayed aloud.

"Dear God please be with Ashley. Help her through this trauma that she's dealing with. Please bring her peace. Dear God help her make the statement she has to make and help her feel your presence."

I sat back and simply laid my arm over her shoulder for several more minutes until her weeping subsided.

"Thank you. Thank you so much, for praying and everything, I mean" she said, looking right into my eyes. I stayed with her as the clock ticked by. Eventually an officer came out to get her and I returned to Delbert. I glanced up at the clock on the wall, which now read 8:50.

"Are you sure you signed me in? I asked worried about the time.

"I'm sure." He said calmly, looking over his reading glasses.

"Look at the clock! I'm not going to be able to get over to the courthouse in time to get my plea in! I'm going to go check, someone must have forgot about us!"

I walked to the window and told her who I was.

"Oh! We wondered where you were! I saw you there and assumed you were with the other girl, I'll let him know you're here."

I sat back down with Delbert. We could hear some sirens going off, I jokingly remarked,

"They're probably all out looking for me- there's a warrant out for my arrest and I didn't turn myself in on time!"

The clock continued to tick by and no one came out to get me. The officer who had gotten the statement from Ashley came over to us, noticing we had been there for hours now, asked,

"Are you being helped?"

I told him who I was and that I was waiting to see Detective Curry. He alerted me that it may be a little longer; he was busy with another case.

He came back out a few minutes later,

"He can see you now." I followed him back to the detective's desk. Detective Curry was very respectful. It was a very relaxed atmosphere, well as relaxed as fingerprinting and mug shots can be! I was handled with a great measure of dignity. We even joked that my husband would use that mug shot for our Christmas card if he got a hold of it! To which he assured me he wouldn't let Delbert near it. An alert came across his radio while we were in the middle of paperwork. His interest perked up as he stopped what he was doing and listened. There had been a car jacking. He had to stop the processing to dispatch officers. It was interesting to be back there and watch him work. But all the chaos made getting to the courthouse early impossible. We wouldn't arrive until after 9:30. When the processing had finally been completed, we were to follow him to the courthouse, several blocks away. As we walked up the courthouse sidewalk, he informed us there would be no citation issued. The officer assigned to do it wasn't in that day, so "we just won't worry about that".

I'm not sure what that was all about but I took it as another 'God thing' I was getting pretty used to them by now! By the time we walked inside to the courtroom area, all three courtrooms were in session. Detective Curry led us into one of them, "I'm not sure what will happen now, but just wait in here until someone calls your name." That was the last time I would see Detective Curry. I would later wish I would have thanked him for how well he had treated me and how respected he had made me feel.

Delbert and I entered the courtroom and to our delight and surprise- there were Minerva and her husband! She hadn't told me she was coming! They had driven nearly as far as we had- just from the opposite direction – to come support me. She simply smiled and stated,

"God and Mary would want me here for you."

We sat there and watched as other court proceedings were going on. Minerva leaned in to talk quietly and it felt so good to have her there. She has a very warm presence that just makes you feel safe. As we were catching up, she got a concerned look on her face.

"I'm not sure about telling the family that I came. I'm not sure how they will take it. You never know how others might be handling their grief. Everyone goes thru the stages at different times."

My questioning expression must have been apparent as I shakily responded,

"You mean there are some who are angry now?"

"I don't know, but I'm just not sure, you know-they could be."

She went on to smile and say something to try to divert me, but I felt as though someone had hit me in the gut. In my euphoria of forgiveness and healing, it never occurred to me that there could be those who wouldn't feel the same now. I cringed at that thought. I couldn't get that thought out of my mind all day, wondering if someone out there was suffering more than I had allowed myself to envision. Every time it entered my mind, tears would come without warning.

The judge, a woman, seemed very compassionate and understanding. as we heard her deal with a reckless driving charge, some driving without license charges, and a few others, her goal was consistent- to get their license reinstated and get them back to work as soon as possible. I was encouraged and anxious to just plead guilty and accept my punishment. But God had a different plan.

We were moved to a different courtroom. This one had a male judge presiding. He presented himself in a much different way. He struck me as tough and no nonsense. We weren't in there long before my name was called.

I stood before him, Minerva at my side, feeling like Dorothy in front of the wizard of Oz, with one of her trusty companions at her side. As I stood below his bench the tears began to fall. They weren't there because of the intimidation. But I was recalling the reason I was there and the finality of Mary's life…and they just fell.

He sat above us, reading through the paperwork in front of him, silently. He then looked up, over his reading glasses and said,

"Where is your attorney?"

"I don't have one, I just want to plead guilty."

"Don't say you want to plead guilty. You need an attorney, these are some serious charges that you're facing!"

"But I just want to plead guilty."

"Don't say that!"

"But I am guilty, I rear-ended her, and she was stopped. I am guilty."

"Will you stop saying that?! Don't you understand the magnitude of these charges? This carries jail time! You really need an attorney!"

"I'm not worried about jail time. I want to take responsibility. I want to plead----

His voice got louder as he interrupted me,

"DO NOT KEEP SAYING THAT! Do not say it again! I'm not just worried about jail time either! A conviction of this magnitude can follow you around for the rest of your life. It will affect insurance rates, employment opportunities; I don't want that for you!

Minerva spoke up,

"Can I speak?"

"Who are you?" he bellowed.

"I'm here on behalf of the victim and the victim's family."

"I don't want to hear from you. I may be the judge who rules on this case; maybe someone else- but this is not the time for you to speak. You will have your chance."

Minerva meekly replied,

"I understand."

I felt so bad for her. She only came to support me and was getting chastised for her efforts

I wanted so badly to explain myself. I felt if he could just hear me out, so again I tried.

"If I could just plead guilty---

Now he was aggravated,

"QUIT SAYING THAT! I'm getting you an attorney! Don't say anything else! I won't hear anything else from you without an attorney present!"

He gave me income paperwork to fill out.

"I think we make too much money to have a public defender" I said as I read what he was handing me.

"What do you make?"

"Well my husband makes over $60,000 a year."

"No, what do you make, just you!"

"Well I raise horses, I don't make anything!" I said with a chuckle, "They eat everything I make!"

"Go back and fill those out- use just your income- and return them back here to me."

I do follow orders well, so I went to the back and filled out the papers, but used our combined income because that's what it asked for, and returned them to the bench.

The judge pointed to a distinguished gray haired man in the courtroom and said,

"This is your attorney! He's the best in the state of Ohio!"

I recognized him from earlier in the day. He had been arguing a case on some precedent and even the judge had seemed impressed with his knowledge and research. He was very well-versed and intelligent, not at all what I would have expected a public defender to be like. We all dispersed into a room outside the courtroom to further discuss my case in a more private setting. He politely opened the door for Delbert and I, but then excused Minerva and her husband.

"No! She stays! They both stay!" I exclaimed.

He rolled his eyes and with a look of dismay, relented.

"Okay, whatever you say."

The tone of his voice showed his disapproval. We sat down at a table with only three chairs, so Minerva and her husband stood against the wall, at the attorney's back. He began by reading over the file in front of him that had the details of my case. As he looked it over I spoke up,

"I just want to plead guilty."

To which he quickly responded, "We're not doing that", not even glancing up as he answered.

"You don't understand. I do not want to plead 'not guilty'- I am guilty!" tearfully and persistently I keep trying to get him to understand.

"I want to be accountable for this, I'm not looking for an out!"

I just wanted to take responsibility, "own up", like I was taught and truly believed I should do, but no one is allowing me to do it! So I continued,

"I rear-ended her, she was totally innocent, her van was stopped. How can I NOT be guilty? Aren't you always guilty when you rear-end someone?

"No, not at all I have represented many people who have rear-ended people who were not at fault." He went on to say, "From what I see here there was no alcohol or drugs, no speeding, no phone use. The state has the burden of proof, they have to prove negligence or intent. Clearly there is no intent and I see no evidence of negligence. What citation was issued?"

"Oh, well they didn't issue one."

"No citation, either?! We're getting you out of this mess!"

I know I should be relieved but I am frustrated at this point. I want to plead guilty because I feel it's right, so I say,

"Can't I still plea bargain and take accountability?"

Perplexed and equally as frustrated he replied,

"I have known this judge for years, we go way back. He will not let you plead guilty today. Why do you think he assigned me to you? I am not a public defender I have my own private practice. I work for his court-room. When he has a case like yours he appoints me to take it, and I don't take them to lose! No, this judge will not let you plead guilty to this and neither would any other judge with an ounce of integrity! This is your only option!"

God is truly amazing! In spite of all my efforts, I could not plead guilty. I went in with no attorney, and no plans to get one, left with an amazing one.

The attorney now set his attention to Minerva.

"So, I suppose you would like to see her get the maximum penalty."

Minerva passionately answered him,

"No! No! No! The minimum, no charges at all if possible! Mary wouldn't want her charged for this!"

The attorney was clearly moved by this,

"Wow! I am so touched! I have done this job for years and have never seen anything like this! The victim's family comes in like this often, but not to support the defendant. That I have never seen! No the family comes in to make sure the defendant gets punished and they always are out for blood! No, nothing like this. I am truly touched- truly!"

He was shaking his head in disbelief as he asked her,

"Could you talk to the prosecutor? I don't think she's in today, but could you come back and let her hear how you feel? That would help a lot!"

"Of course we will, of course! Whatever we can do!" she seemed excited to be of some help.

"Yes, touching, truly touching," he said as we all stood to go back before the judge.

Upon entering the courtroom, the attorney exclaimed,

"Hey, look! There she is, that's the prosecutor over there!"

The lawyers got together and spoke briefly and the prosecutor came over to see Minerva and Freeman. They went out of the room to speak privately. After a short time, Minerva came rushing back into the courtroom. She enthusiastically and jubilantly said in a voice probably too loud for a courtroom setting,

"She's a Christian! She's a Christian! It's going to be alright!"

The passion was pouring out of her as she rejoiced for me! What an amazing friend I have found! I knew God had sent her to me, but each time I see her that is reaffirmed.

Minerva went on to explain how their conversation had went. The prosecutor had asked her what she wanted to see done, if she wanted me punished by whatever means the law would allow. Minerva had told her that she represented Mary, and she would never want that. They were there to advocate for the lightest possible punishment, if there had to be one at all. This lawyer was just as taken back as the last as they heard the grace poured out on my behalf. A pre-trial date was set for a month later and Minerva had said she would make the long trip again to see this thru to the end. The four of us had a long lunch, sharing stories of Mary and family and getting to know our new friends a little better.

Delbert and I spent yet another car ride home marveling of the wonder of our God. God always shows up, though we do not deserve it. He shows up, even when we try to sabotage His grace-if we pray and seek His will in our lives. He shows up! Praise God, He always shows up!

The following month went by quickly. I communicated with Minerva almost every day. Usually by face book or text. We were becoming fast friends. There were hard times for her that she would briefly share. I'm certain she didn't want me to feel bad for her loss, but I knew she missed her dear friend and confidante. Mary had a birthday within the beginning of our friendship. I cried for Minerva and Mary's family, as I was sure that day was difficult for many. I had kept busy telling and retelling Mary's wonderful story of grace poured out to me on her behalf. I thought often about the legacy she left behind, hoping mine might be even just a portion of hers.

As the pre-trial day approached, I received a message from Minerva. "I thought I should warn you, Barbara might be calling you soon."

Barbara is Mary's sister. I was so excited to get to hear from her! I answered my phone with high hopes every time the phone rang! A couple days went by without a word, then one evening my voicemail ring tone went off! That was strange, I thought, my phone didn't ring. I had it on me at all times awaiting her call. When I listened to the voicemail, it was Barbara's voice I heard! I was so eager to talk to her so I pushed the number to return the call. To my disappointment I got her voicemail. I left a brief message but I was extremely disheartened. I had hoped that she was asking about the pre trial. I so wanted to see her again! I went back to my voicemail to try to listen for her number so I could write it down. For whatever reason, my phone had no record of the call coming in on my history, so the only way to get the number was through the voicemail that she had left. As I listened to her voicemail in my enthusiasm, I inadvertently deleted the message instead of saving it. I was distraught! I quickly called my cell phone carrier and asked them to look it up. She tried but was having no luck either. Baffled, she kept me on the line for nearly a half hour and had pretty much given up, when a call started to come thru.

"It's her! It's her! She's trying to call me now! It's her I'm hanging up now I got to take this!" I shouted as excited as I had been the night I was told I could attend the funeral.

It was her.

"Hello, Tracy? This is Barbara, Mary's sister. Do you remember me?"

"Yes! Yes! Of course I do! It's so good to hear from you! I can't tell you how glad I am that you called!" I exclaimed.

"I have wanted to call and just see how you are doing, but things have been so busy here, you know how it is. So, how are you doing?" Barbara replied.

"I am wonderful! The funeral, Mary's family- your family- you have made all the difference! The love you all showed me, the forgiveness, I can't even tell you what it has meant! It was just amazing- you all are so amazing!" Joy filled my tone a I answered.

"It was important for all of us as well you know, meeting you and everything." Barbara stated.

"How have you been, with Mary gone, how has it been for you?" I was afraid to ask the question, but I really wanted to know.

"Not too bad. It's strange, but life has been crazy since that day and I haven't had much time to sit and think. But I miss her, of course I miss her."

I was sure she was sparing my feelings. I shouldn't have asked. We went on and talked for a while and she eventually asked about the pre trial.

"Do you want to come? I really think you should be there. Whatever your position is- you have a right to voice it to the court. Where are you located? We could come and get you, I'll look it up and see how far it is for us."

I looked it up while I had her on the phone. She was two or more hours the other side of where the courthouse was from us. I had thought she may have been, because I heard Minerva say they lived close to each other at one time.

"We could still come to get you, it's far for us, but we want you there."

I had mentioned Minerva to her but didn't want to volunteer her. But Barbara had decided to hang up with me to try to find another way to get there. She called back not too long later and had made arrangements for her brother to take her. She had mentioned that he had to miss a full days work to do it and didn't seem too eager. In the meantime I had sent a text to Minerva and she had told me that Barbara wasn't far out of her way and she would be glad to bring her. Well eventually after a little effort, arrangements were made and Barbara and her husband were to join Minerva to make the trip to the courthouse the following day. And I couldn't wait!

Once again Delbert and I made the trip past that forsaken stretch of highway where so long ago this whirlwind journey had started. Again we arrived an hour early, but this time I was expecting our new dear, dear friends. Once we arrived and found the room where the pre trial was to be held. I contacted Minerva to see if they had arrived. They were sitting in the parking lot, waiting to come in.

"They're here! They're just outside!" I was so thrilled to see them again! They came up to the waiting area outside the courtroom, I watched for them and as they walked down the hall, I hurried to greet them. We embraced and smiled, equally as happy to see each other. We sat and talked for almost the entire hour, as time flew by, Barbara sharing more delightful stories of Mary. I could hear them all day! She was truly a remarkable lady! As we sat there I recognized my attorney walk by with another client. He nods and says something like, "Oh good you're here already." And then hurries on. I didn't mind him being preoccupied, the conversation was refreshing and I didn't really want it to end.

It wasn't long before he came back into view and motioned me to follow him. We went into the courtroom and sat at a table. He went over the proposal put together by the prosecutor.

"It's a pretty sweet deal. You plead 'no contest' and they give you the minimum fine of $500 and a year driver's license suspension, with a ton of privileges! They are giving you weekend allowances, as well as work related, medical related, court related like I said, a pretty sweet deal!"

I was very happy with what he was telling me. I never wanted to plead not guilty so this is what I wanted all along!

"Let me ask you this, I have worship practice at the church. I'm on the worship team, but we don't get paid, would volunteer work count as work?"

He must have misunderstood, because in a loud, annoyed voice he said,

"This is a great deal, they are cutting you a big break and you want to go in there and ask for more? Do you realize when you plead 'guilty' or even 'no contest' to this charge there is more often than not jail time associated with this?"

"Oh no! I'm not complaining, and I'm not asking to change a thing! I just want to know exactly what it means so I don't break any of the rules! I am very happy with the terms, that's not what I meant at all!"

He still appeared somewhat disgruntled to me and I wished I would not have asked. He showed me where to sign and we walked back outside and I joined the others once again. I let them know the terms that we had agreed to. I told them I was very happy with it and they seemed to be as well.

We were called into the courtroom in short order. The judge read the conditions as the attorney and I stood before his bench. He no longer seemed a threatening figure, I saw him as kind and just. When he had finished going through the legalities of the plea, he asked if there was anyone in the courtroom who wanted to speak. Minerva stood up and told of Mary and what she had meant to her. She had tears as she talked of how she would miss her, but that Mary would not want me punished for this accident. He asked if there was anyone else?

Barbara arose and took her place in front of the bench.

"I am Barbara, Mary was my sister", she said in a voice as meek and mild as a child, "and it would make my life so much easier if she would get the least possible. I would like her not to be punished at all."

Their abundant love was impacting the judge the same way it had touched everyone else privileged enough to witness it. I believe he was choking back his own tears as he answered her request.

"This is as good as I can do. This is the least we can give in these circumstances. But I really want to thank you for coming and saying what you have. We, in the court system, do not get to see things like this, people like you, very often. Actually, in all my years on the bench I have never seen it before. It's very special what you have done, very moving."

My attorney spoke up:

"Um, there is one more thing you could do. We would like church privileges added, if you would."

"Absolutely! Church privileges" he repeats, as he adds it to the documents.

As I looked around, it struck me. This is Mary's story, her legacy. This family truly honored her in her passing and impacted everyone involved. The courtroom was filled with people who had the privilege of seeing love and forgiveness at work. Attorneys on both sides were fighting back tears. My life was changed forever. Once again my husband and I were in awe at the wonders of God. Only He can turn tragedy into triumph. I have come to expect nothing less.

Post script: I now have a huge expanded family. Barbara introduces me as her sister. I have gotten very close with both her and Paul without them this book would not have come to fruition.